AN ENEMY
OF THE PEOPLE,
THE WILD DUCK

NOTES

including
- *Introduction and Biography*
- *Brief Summaries*
- *Act-by-Act Summaries and Commentaries*
- *Critical Notes and Character Analyses*
- *Questions for Discussion*
- *Selected Bibliography*

by
Marianne Sturman

INCORPORATED

LINCOLN, NEBRASKA 68501

Editor

Gary Carey, M.A.
University of Colorado

Consulting Editor

James L. Roberts, Ph.D.
Department of English
University of Nebraska

ISBN 0-8220-0617-0
© Copyright 1965
by
C. K. Hillegass
All Rights Reserved
Printed in U.S.A.

1989 Printing

Cliffs Notes, Inc.   Lincoln, Nebraska

CONTENTS

INTRODUCTION

Once the subject of public controversy, defended only by the *avant-garde* theater critics of the nineteenth century, Ibsen's prose dramas now appear as successful television plays and are an essential part of the repertory theaters all over the world. No longer inflaming audience reactions, the dramas are now acceptable fare to the most conservative theatergoer.

Because Ibsenite drama has become part of the history of the theater, a study of his work gives us a special insight into contemporary writings. The modern "theater of the absurd," for instance, expressing a personal alienation from society, is merely another form of the social criticism which Ibsen first inspired.

With this in mind, these synopses of Ibsen's *The Wild Duck, Ghosts,* and *An Enemy of the People* and their accompanying critical commentaries are designed to help the student rediscover the significance of Ibsen's work and to guide him in evaluating the contemporary appeal — if any — of his drama.

The purpose of these Notes is to amplify the student's understanding of the plays; by no means can this booklet substitute the esthetic and emotional satisfaction to be gained from reading the plays themselves. Because Ibsen's dramas lend themselves to a variety of interpretations, the student should feel encouraged to develop his own critical approach to Ibsen from reading this volume. Designed to encourage discussion between the student and the critic represented in this writing, the Notes should be merely used as a basis for a critical dialogue. The plays themselves must supply the intellectual stimulation.

A BRIEF BIOGRAPHY OF IBSEN

Henrik Ibsen's ancestors were sea captains and businessmen, while his father was a well-to-do merchant, dealing chiefly in lumber. Ibsen was born in 1828 in Skien, a town in the south of Norway. Three brothers and a sister were born after him, but Henrik was the only member of his family to show any promise. When he was eight years old, his father's business failed and the family retired to a country house. Ibsen bitterly recalled how their friends, eager to dine and drink as guests of the affluent merchant, forsook all connections with the Ibsens when they lost their financial standing.

Although the young Ibsen showed talent as a painter, his family was too poor to allow him to study art; neither could they afford to train him for his chosen profession in medicine. When he was fifteen, his father sent him to Grimstad, a small provincial town south of Skien. Here he became an apothecary's apprentice, the next best thing to medicine. In the first three years of his Grimstad life, Ibsen lived entirely alone. Too uncommunicative to make friends and too poor to seek entertainments, he read voraciously, particularly in contemporary poetry and in theology. Eventually he was the center of a small circle of young men, and during this time began to write poetry.

Learning Latin in order to prepare for the university, Ibsen studied Cicero and became deeply interested in the character of Catiline, the agitator and revolutionary who was eventually assassinated. His first play, a historical drama in verse, was an attempt to explain this elusive character. *Catiline,* however, when published at the private expense of one enthusiastic friend, received no public notice and few copies were sold.

After six dark years in the hostile atmosphere of this provincial Norwegian village, Ibsen, by extreme economy and privation, had saved enough money to leave for the capital, Christiania (Oslo). Hoping to study at the university, he enrolled in a "student factory," a popular name given to an irregular school which coached students for the entrance examinations. Here Ibsen first met his lifelong rival and contemporary, Björnstjerne Björnson, who was to be known in the future, along with Ibsen, as a national poet of Norway. Found deficient in two subjects, Ibsen failed to enter the university. At this time as well, *Catiline* was rejected by the Christiania theater, but his *The Warrior's Barrow* was accepted and performed three times in 1850.

At this period of Ibsen's youth, Norway experienced a nationalist awakening. The new literary generation, after four hundred years of Danish rule (1397-1818), sought to revive the glories of Norwegian history and medieval literature. The middle ages were glorified as well because the romantic movement was in full swing throughout Europe. Thus, when Ole Bull, the great violinist, founded a Norse theater at Bergen, the project met with enthusiastic approval from all the youthful idealists eager to subvert the influence of Danish culture.

At a benefit performance to raise money for the new venture, Ibsen presented the prologue — a poem glorifying Norway's past — which moved Ole Bull to appoint him theater poet and stage manager of the Bergen theater. This position launched Ibsen on his dramatic career. Staging more than 150 plays, including works by Shakespeare and the French dramatist Scribe, Ibsen gained as much practical experience in stagecraft as that possessed by Shakespeare and Moliére. In addition to his managerial position, the poet was obliged to produce one original play a year. Although his *The Warrior's Barrow* and *St. John's Night* met with failure, the critics approved of *Lady Inger of Ostratt* (1855) and *The Feast of Solhaug* (1856). In this same year, the twenty-eight year old Ibsen became engaged to Susannah Thoresen, a girl of strong personality and independent judgment, and the marriage took place two years later.

Encouraged by the success of Ole Bull's Norse theater in Bergen, enthusiasts of nationalist poetry in the capital also founded a new theater in direct competition with the conservative, Danish-influenced Christiania theater. Asked to direct this new venture, Ibsen's promised salary was twice the amount he received at Bergen, about six hundred specie dollars.

Returning to the capital with a new play, *The Vikings at Helgeland,* Ibsen first submitted the manuscript to the old Christiania theater where he would be free to collect royalties. At first the Danish director accepted the piece; but returned it a few months later with a flimsy excuse. This gratuitous insult sparked a hot controversy between Ibsen, Björnson, and their followers on the one hand, and the adherents of the Danish influence on the other. After five years of public controversy, the conservative director was forced to resign, while *The Vikings* became one of the chief pieces performed under the theater's new management.

Throughout these early years, the relationship between Ibsen and Björnson was very friendly. Björnson became godfather when the Ibsens' son, Sigurd, was born in 1859; when the dramatist was in serious financial straits, Björnson made every effort to raise money for him. The two men also shared the same circle of friends at this time, although Ibsen was disappointed to find that his poetic ideals were misunderstood by his gregarious contemporaries. In a poem, *On the Heights,* he expressed the view that a man who wishes to devote himself to the arts must sacrifice the usual pleasures of life; a poet must view life apart in order to find in it models for his work.

Ibsen suffered great depression during this part of his life. The varied responsibilities of his job allowed him no chance for his own creative work. In addition, the theater was doing so badly that his salary was severely reduced. Besides neglecting his work, he published no play from 1857 until *Love's Comedy* in 1862. This new anti-romantic satire received hostile reviews although it shows a maturing talent and the bold viewpoint which characterizes his later works. When the theater finally declared bankruptcy, Ibsen's despair was complete. Like Captain Alving, he became a victim of that "second-rate town which had no joys to offer—only dissipations," and spent much time in barrooms. Björnson, meanwhile, was a successful and already famous poet to whom the government awarded an annual grant of four hundred dollars to devote himself exclusively to poetic works. However Ibsen's fortunes changed in the following year when *The Pretenders,* a play glorifying the Norse heroes of the past, won an enthusiastic reception from both audience and reviewers. As a result of this success, the government awarded Ibsen a travelling scholarship to bring him in contact with the cultural trends in the rest of Europe.

Visiting Rome, Ibsen viewed for the first time the great art masterpieces of the classical and renaissance periods. In the warm, sunny climate of Italy, Ibsen felt intoxicated with his freedom from the stultifying atmosphere of Norwegian provincialism. Retiring with his family to a little town in the hills, Ibsen wrote with an inspired pen. Affected by the events of the Prusso-Danish war over Schleswig-Holstein, his interests turning from the esthetic to the ethical, Ibsen produced the colossal *Brand*.

Considered "the most stirring event in Norway's literary history of the nineteenth century," this drama won nationwide fame for its author. The protagonist of the play, a mystical clergyman, is a courageous idealist of noble stature whose lack of love for humanity destroys his wife and child in an uncompromising commitment to his ethical principles.

Published in the following year, *Peer Gynt* established Ibsen's international fame. This exuberant, fantasy-filled drama is the antithesis of *Brand*. The spoiled darling of a weak mother and rich father, Peer lives according to the principle of "to thyself — enough." Rather than overcoming obstacles, he goes "roundabout" and avoids facing problems. Unlike Brand, Peer never commits himself to principles unless they are to his personal benefit. The play is full of symbolic allusions and rich lyrical poetry. In 1867, the king decorated Ibsen for his achievement.

After four years in Italy, Ibsen settled down to his lifework, first in Dresden and then in Munich. His biography from this point on is more or less uneventful. Producing a new play every two years, Ibsen's dramatic powers increased and his social criticism ripened. Along with Björnson, he was considered Norway's greatest poet, but he maintained primacy as a dramatist. Honors heaped upon him and with a prosperous income, Ibsen appeared as a frock-coated and respectable middle class individual.

Almost entirely self-inspired, Ibsen was a rare genius who required no outside influence for his work. Unlike Björnson who lectured, made frequent public appearances and wrote novels and plays as well as poems, Ibsen kept to himself as much as possible. Constantly working and reworking his dramas throughout each two year period, rarely divulging, even to his family, the nature of his current writing, he single-mindedly pursued his art. Just as he gave up painting in his youth for writing poetry and drama, he now stopped composing poems, eventually relinquishing even the verse form of his earlier plays for the prose of the later works.

Harsh self-analysis was one of his life principles. In each play he expresses this constant introspection, always underscoring a thesis based on self-seeking. In *Emperor and Galilean*, for example, Julian fails to establish the "first empire" of pagan sensuality, then casts aside the "second empire" of Christian self-abnegation. As the hero expires, he envisions a "third empire," where, in the words of the biographer Zucker, "men were to find God not on Mount Olympus nor on Calvary but in their own souls, wills, and senses." Ibsen himself once wrote in a poem, that "to live is to fight with trolls in heart and brain. To be a poet is to pronounce a final judgment upon oneself."

The British commentator, Francis Bull, sums up Ibsen's personal search:

> More deeply than ordinary men, Ibsen was split in two—a great genius and a shy and timid little philistine. In daily life he quite often did not come up to his own heroic ideals and revolutionary theories, but listened to the troll voices of narrow-minded egotism and compromise—and then, afterwards, the genius in him arose, a judge without mercy. This ever-recurring fight meant to him lifelong suffering; but it was this drama constantly going on in his own soul that made him a great dramatist and compelled him again and again to undertake a penetrating self-analysis.

Ibsen died in 1906. His tombstone, inscribed only with a hammer, the miner's symbol, alludes to a poem Ibsen wrote as a youth. Ending with "Break me the way, you heavy hammer,/ To the deepest bottom of my heart," the verse is a succinct statement of the intensity of Ibsen's personal vision and of his dramatic art.

FIVE PLAYS BY IBSEN: A BRIEF SUMMARY

Ibsen's most famous plays include *A Doll's House, Hedda Gabler, Ghosts, An Enemy of the People,* and *The Wild Duck.* For the analyses of the plays not included in this volume, see the companion volume on Ibsen, published by Cliffs Notes.

A DOLL'S HOUSE

Norma Helmer once secretly borrowed a large sum of money so that her husband could recuperate from a serious illness. She never told him of this loan and has been secretly paying it back in small installments by saving from her household allowance. Her husband, Torvald, thinks her careless and childlike, and often calls her his doll. When he is appointed bank director, his first act is to relieve a man who was once disgraced for having forged his signature on a document. This man, Nils Krogstad, is the person from whom Nora has borrowed her money. It is then revealed that she forged her father's signature in order to get the money. Krogstad threatens to reveal Nora's crime and thus disgrace her and her husband unless Nora can convince her husband not to fire him. Nora tries to influence her husband, but he thinks of Nora as a simple child who cannot understand the value of money or business. Thus, when Helmer discovers that Nora has forged her father's name, he is ready to disclaim his wife even though she had done it for him. Later when all is solved, Nora sees that her husband is not worth her love and she leaves him.

HEDDA GABLER

Hedda, the daughter of the famous General Gabler, married George Tesman out of desperation. But she found life with him to be dull and tedious. During their wedding trip, her husband spent most of his time in libraries doing research in history for a book that is soon to be published. He is hoping to receive a position in the university.

An old friend of Hedda's comes to visit her and tells her of Eilert Lövborg, an old friend of both women. Eilert Lövborg has also written a book on history that is highly respected. In the past, however, he has lived a life of degeneration. Now he has quit drinking and has devoted himself to serious work. His new book has all the imagination and spirit that is missing in George Tesman's book. Hedda's friend, Thea Elvsted, tells how she has helped Eilert stop drinking and begin constructive work.

Later at a visit, Lövborg is offered a drink. He refuses and Hedda, jealous over the influence that Thea has on Lövborg, tempts him into taking a drink. He then goes to a party where he loses his manuscript. When George Tesman returns home with Lövborg's manuscript, Hedda burns it because she is jealous of it. Later, Lövborg comes to her and confesses how he has failed in his life. Hedda talks him into committing suicide by shooting himself in the temple. Lövborg does commit suicide later but it is through a wound in the stomach. George then begins to reconstruct Lövborg's manuscript with the help of notes provided by Thea Elvsted. Suddenly, Hedda leaves the room, takes her pistols and commits suicide.

GHOSTS

Mrs. Alving is building an orphanage as a memorial to her husband. This edifice is to be dedicated the next day, and her old friend Parson Manders has come to perform the ceremonies. In a private conversation, Mrs. Alving tells the Parson that her husband had been a complete degenerate, and she is using the rest of his money to build the orphanage so that she can leave only *her* money to her son Oswald, who has just arrived home from years and years abroad.

In a private talk with his mother, Oswald confesses that he has an incurable disease which the doctors think was inherited. Oswald, however, believes his father to have been a perfect man. Mrs. Alving, then, must confess that Mr. Alving had indeed been a degenerated man and that Oswald caught the disease from his father. Oswald knows that he is dying and wants to take the maid as his mistress so that the maid, Regina, will give him poison when he is next struck by the disease. Mrs. Alving then explains that Regina is in reality his half sister. This does not bother Oswald, but Regina refuses to stay. Oswald then tells his mother that she must administer the medicine when the next attack comes. As the play closes, Oswald begins to have his attack and his mother does not know whether to administer the poison or to endure the agony.

AN ENEMY OF THE PEOPLE

Dr. Stockmann has discovered that the new baths built in his town are infected with a deadly disease and instructs the town to repair or close the baths. The Mayor, who is Dr. Stockmann's brother, does not believe the report and refuses to close the baths because it will cause the financial ruin of the town.

Dr. Stockmann tries to take his case to the people, but the mayor intercedes and explains to the people how much it will cost to repair the baths. He explains that the Doctor is always filled with wild, fanciful ideas. In a public meeting, he has his brother declared an enemy of the people. The doctor decides to leave the town, but at the last minute comes to the realization that he must stay and fight for the things he believes to be right.

THE WILD DUCK

Gregers Werle has avoided his father, whom he detests, by spending fifteen years in the family mining concern. Gregers is so unattractive in appearance that he has given up all hope of marrying and having a family; instead, he has become an idealist and goes about advocating and preaching a theme of truth and purity. He calls his mission the "claim of the ideal."

His father, Old Werle, has allegedly driven his sick wife to her death by carrying on love affairs in his own home. He had once had his serving girl, Gina, as his mistress. Arranging her marriage with Hialmar Ekdal, the son of his former partner, Werle also sets the couple up in the profession of photography. Hialmar is pleased with his marriage and believes that Gina's child is his own daughter. At present, Old Werle lives with his housekeeper and between them there are no secrets.

Lieutenant Ekdal, Werle's former partner, is now a broken old man. He does odd jobs for Werle. Earlier, the company had appropriated a large quantity of lumber from a government owned farm. Werle placed all the blame on Ekdal who was sentenced to prison. He is now living with Hialmar and Gina.

Gregers Werle comes to Hialmar and explains the claim of the ideal and tries to make Hialmar see that his marriage is based on a lie. But rather than making Hialmar happy by understanding the true nature of his marriage, Gregers only succeeds in turning Halmar against his daughter, Hedvig. The daughter, in order to prove her love for her father who is rejecting her, takes a pistol and kills herself. Hialmar then becomes bitterly remorseful about his behavior.

GHOSTS

ACT I

Summary
Regina Enstrand, a young girl in service for Mrs. Alving, appears in the garden. She tries to prevent her father, Jacob Engstrand, from entering. The rain makes the old man even more disreputable looking than usual, and Regina makes it clear she is ashamed of his coarseness and vulgar appearance. Engstrand has come to ask Regina to live with him and work for him in his planned "seamen's home." He says he has saved enough money from doing carpentry work on the new orphanage to begin this enterprise and now that she has grown into "such a fine wench" she would be a valuable asset. He clearly implies that this seamen's home will be a high class brothel. Regina says she has her own plans for the future, especially since Oswald Alving has just returned from his studies in Paris.

Pastor Manders enters after Engstrand has left. He talks with Regina about her father. Since Engstrand requires a strong influence to keep him from drinking, Manders suggests that Regina, out of filial duty, return to live with him and be "the guiding hand" in her father's life. Regina says she would rather seek a place in town as a governess.

While the girl goes to fetch Mrs. Alving, Manders peruses some books on the table. He gives a start after reading the title page of one, and with increasing disapproval looks at some others. Cordially and affectionately, Mrs. Alving comes in to greet him. Politely inquiring after Oswald, Manders then asks who reads these books. Shocked to find they are hers, he wonders how such readings could contribute to her feeling of self-reliance, as she puts it, or how they can confirm her own impressions. What is objectionable about the books, she asks. "I have read quite enough about them to disapprove of them," he answers. "But your own opinion—" she pursues. He talks as if to a child:

> My dear Mrs. Alving, there are many occasions in life when one has to rely on the opinions of others. That is the way in the world, and it is quite right that it should be so. What would become of society otherwise?

He now wishes to discuss their mutual business—the Captain Alving Orphanage—built by Mrs. Alving in honor of her late husband. Although she has left all the arrangements to Manders, he wants to ask whether they should insure the buildings. To her prompt "of course," he raises objections since the orphanage is dedicated to "higher causes." He points out that his fellow clergymen and their congregations might interpret the insurance to mean "that neither you nor I had a proper reliance on Divine protection." As Mrs. Alving's advisor he himself would be the first attacked by "spiteful persons" who would publicly slander him. She assures him that under these conditions she would not wish the buildings insured.

Speaking of insurance, Mrs. Alving mentions that the building nearly caught fire yesterday from some burning shavings in the carpenter's shop. She says she has heard that Engstrand is often careless with matches. Manders makes excuses because the "poor fellow" has so many anxieties. "Heaven be thanked," he says, "I am told he is really making an effort to live a blameless life…Why he assured me so himself." Manders thinks it would be best for Engstrand if Regina returned to live with him, but Mrs. Alving's firm "No!" is definitive.

Oswald appears, bearing so much likeness to his dead father that Manders is startled; Mrs. Alving quickly insists that her son takes after her. During their conversation, Oswald shocks the pastor by depicting the fidelity and beauty of family life among the common-law marriages of his fellow painters in Paris. Dissapproving of artists in the first place, Manders sputters indignantly at such circles "where open immorality is rampant." He cannot understand how "the authorities would tolerate such things" and is even more dismayed when Mrs. Alving later declares that Oswald "was right in every single word he said." In her loneliness, she continues, she has come to the same conclusions as her son, that the married men of good social standing are capable of the greatest acts of immorality.

It is his duty to speak now, but not just as a friend, Manders says, "it is your priest that stands before you just as he once did at the most critical moment of your life." He reminds her how she came to him after the first year of marriage, refusing to return to her husband. She softly reminds him that the first year was "unspeakably unhappy." To crave for happiness is simply to be "possessed by a spirit of revolt," he answers. Bound in marriage by a "sacred bond" her duty was "to cleave to the man you had chosen;" though a husband be profligate, a wife's duty is to bear the cross laid upon her shoulders by "a higher will," Manders continues. It was imprudent for her to have sought refuge with him at the time, and he is proud to have had the strength of character to lead her back "to the path of duty" and back to her husband.

Having defaulted in her wifely duty, she also neglected her duty as a mother, Manders goes on. Because she sent Oswald to boarding schools all his life rather than educating him at home, the child has become a thorough profligate. "In very truth, Mrs. Alving, you are a guilty mother!" Manders exhorts.

These conclusions are unjust, Mrs. Alving answers, for Manders knew nothing of her life from that moment on. He must know now "that my husband died just as great a profligate as he had been all his life." In fact, she tells him, a disease he contracted from his lifelong excesses caused his death. Manders gropes for a chair. To think that all the years of her wedded life were nothing but "a hidden abyss of misery" makes his brain reel. She says that her husband's scandalous conduct invaded the walls of this very house for she witnessed Alving's approaches to the servant Joanna. "My husband had his will of that girl," Mrs. Alving continues, "and that intimacy had consequences." Only later on does Manders discover that the "consequences" are Regina.

Mrs. Alving goes on to describe how she sat up with her husband during his drinking bouts, being his companion so he would not leave the house to seek others. She had to listen to his ribald talk and then, with brute force, bring him to bed. She endured all this for Oswald's sake, sending him to boarding schools when he was old enough to ask questions. As long as his father was alive, Oswald never set foot in his home.

Besides thoughts of her son, she also had her work to sustain her, Mrs. Alving tells Manders. Too besotted to be useful, her husband depended on her to keep him in touch with his work during his lucid intervals. She improved and arranged all his properties, and she is converting his share of the estate into the "Captain Alving Orphanage." By this gesture Mrs. Alving hopes to "silence all rumors and clear away all doubt" as to the truth of her husband's life. None of his father's estate shall pass on to Oswald; "my son shall have everything from me," she states.

Grumbling at "this everlasting rain," Oswald returns from his walk. When Regina announces that dinner is ready, Oswald follows her into the dining room to uncork the wines. Meanwhile Manders and Mrs. Alving discuss the dedication ceremony for the opening of the orphange tomorrow. She regards the occasion as the end of "this long dreadful comedy." After tomorrow she shall feel as if the dead husband had never lived here. Then "there will be no one else here but my boy and his mother," she declares. They hear a quiet scuffle from the next room, then Regina's whisper, "Oswald! Are you mad? Let me go!" Horror-struck, Mrs. Alving hoarsely whispers to Manders, "Ghosts. The couple in the conservatory—over again." He is bewildered. Then knowledge dawns. "What are you saying! Regina—? Is she—?" His hostess nods helplessly. The curtain comes down.

Commentary

As the first act functions to introduce the characters, the central problem of the play, as well as the essential story line, the playwright carefully forewarns his audience of the themes he will develop in subsequent acts. In fact, the first scene of a well written drama often presents a complete analogy of the whole play. With this in mind, the author imparts special significance to the order of appearance of his characters.

Regina is the first to appear, showing by dress and demeanor that she is a properly reared servant maid. As she talks with her father, the audience recognizes that, though she is of vulgar stock, she has aspirations to gentility. This is shown as she uses her little knowledge of French.

Engstrand's appearance keynotes the theme of a depraved parent who ensnares his child in his own dissolution, especially as the carpenter asks Regina to join him in his planned enterprise. Implying that she is not his true-born daughter, Ibsen also introduces the theme that children, although unaware of their origins, inherit qualities from their parents. As Regina accuses her father of being able to "humbug" the reverend, and later on showing how Manders accepts Engstrand's hypocrisy for fact, Ibsen introduces the idea that society recognizes phrase-mongering rather than integrity of thought and action as a standard of moral respectability.

Pastor Manders appears next; suggesting that Regina return to live with her father shows how he allies himself with Jacob Engstrand. The respectability and social orthodoxy which he expresses in phrases like "daughter's duty" rather then defining his principles through thoughtful investigations, show that Manders supports anyone whose cant agrees with his own.

After Manders peruses the books, Mrs. Alving enters. The audience senses that she is separated from the pastor by an abyss created by her intellect and experience, as symbolized by the books. Arranged on the table which stands between them, these volumes are in fact their first subject of dissension. One does not have to read them to denounce them, Manders states. He is content to accept the opinions of others. By her answers, Mrs. Alving shows she is no longer satisfied by dogma; she must learn truth through her own experience.

Since Manders indicates no ability to learn anything not expressed in pious formulas, we cannot expect his character to change during the drama. Mrs. Alving, on the other hand, welcoming controversy and opposing the results of her experience to what she has always been taught, is fully prepared to face the full impact of events forthcoming in the rest of the play. This quality marks Mrs. Alving as the protagonist of the drama. Having established these intellectual qualities of the mother, Ibsen now brings forth Oswald. As the entire product of Mrs. Alving's life, he presents the greatest problem she will confront.

This arrangement of character introduction suggests the opposing tensions of the play. Regina, her dead mother, and Engstrand parallel Oswald, his mother, and the dead Mr. Alving. One side represents that part of society whose members have loose morals, aspirations to gentility, and who grab at whatever opportunity for self-betterment they can; the other side represents the best in society, a group whose members are cultured, propertied, and have strong ethics. In the middle, as if he were a fulcrum balancing the extremes, stands Pastor Manders. Already appearing as a moralizing but empty-headed standard of society, denouncing Mrs. Alving's intellectual inquiry and supporting Engstrand's hypocrisy, the character of Manders allows the audience to foresee the thesis of the drama: that a society which unwittingly destroys individuality and encourages deceit perpetrates disease — physical as well as emotional — upon its youthful members.

ACT II

Summary

The scene is unchanged, but now it has stopped raining and a mist obscures the outside landscape. With dinner finished, Oswald out for a walk, and Regina busy with the laundry, Mrs. Alving and Manders continue their conversation. She tells how she managed to hush up the scandal of Alving's conduct by providing Joanna with a handsome dowry and having her respectably married off to Jacob Engstrand. Manders is shocked that the carpenter lied to him by confessing of his "light behavior" with Joanna and so deceived the pastor to perform the ceremony. How could a man, "for a paltry seventy pounds" allow himself to be bound in marriage "to a fallen woman." Mrs. Alving points out that she was married to a "fallen man," but Manders says the two cases are as different as night and day. Yes, his hostess agrees, there was a great difference in the price paid, "between a paltry seventy pounds and a whole fortune"; besides, her family arranged the marriage, for she was in love with someone else at the time. To answer her meaningful glance, Manders weakly concludes that at least the match was made "in complete conformity with law and order." I often think that law and order are "at the bottom of all the misery in the world," retorts Mrs. Alving. She regrets her lifelong cowardice. Were she not such a coward in the name of law and order, she says, "I would have told Oswald all I have told you, from beginning to end." Manders points out that she taught her son to idealize his father and as a mother she must feel forbidden to shatter his illusions. "And what about the truth?" asks Mrs. Alving. "What about his ideals?" responds Manders, underlining Ibsen's basic equation that "ideals" equal "lies".

Although Mrs. Alving wishes to quickly find a post for Regina before Oswald gets her in trouble, she regrets her cowardice. To prevent further deceit she should rather encourage the marriage or any other arrangement, she tells the pastor. Manders is shocked that she can suggest a relationship based on incest; as to her so-called cowardice, he denies there was any better way to tell Oswald of his father. By being a coward, Mrs. Alving explains, she succumbs to ghosts:

> I am frightened and timid because I am obsessed by the presence of ghosts that I never can get rid of...When I heard Regina and Oswald in there it was just like seeing ghosts before my eyes. I am half inclined to think we are all ghosts, Mr. Manders. It is not only what we have inherited from our fathers and mothers that exists again in us, but all sorts of old dead ideas and all kinds of old dead beliefs and things of that kind. They are not actually alive in us, but there they are dormant all the

same, and we can never be rid of them. Whenever I take up a newspaper and read it I fancy I see ghosts creeping between the lines. There must be ghosts all over the world. They must be countless as the grains of the sands, it seems to me. And we are so miserably afraid of the light, all of us.

Manders blames these strange ideas on her reading—this "subversive, free-thinking literature"—but she says her ideas come from suffering what Manders himself praised "as right and just what my whole soul revolted against as it would against something abominable." You think it was wrong for me to entreat you as a wife to return to your lawful husband "when you came to me half distracted and crying, 'Here I am, take me!' " asks the pastor. "I think it was," she answers.

Manders declares he can no longer allow a young girl to remain in her house and Regina must go home to her father's care. At this moment there is a knock at the door. Engstrand enters, respectfully requesting the reverend to lead "all of us who have worked so honestly together" on the orphanage building in some concluding prayers. Closely questioning Engstrand about his marriage and other matters, Manders offers the carpenter a chance to explain what must "lie so heavy" on his conscience. The old man makes a fine show of piousness and sensitive feelings as he tells his story. Manders, with tears in his eyes at his flawless life, offers Engstrand a strong handshake of faith and friendship. The pastor, turning to his hostess, asks if she doesn't think that we must be "exceedingly careful" before "condemning our fellow men." "What I think is that you are, and always will remain, a big baby, Mr. Manders," she answers, and thinks that "I should like to give you a big hug!" Hurriedly, the pastor goes out to conduct the prayer meeting.

Discovering Oswald in the dining room, Mrs. Alving sits down with him for a chat. Her son complains that, besides being constantly tired, the lack of sunshine prevents him from painting. This is no ordinary fatigue, he tells his mother, but it is part of a sickness a Paris doctor diagnosed for him. He was told he had this "canker of disease" since his birth. Oswald continues that "the old cynic said, 'The sins of the fathers are visited on the children'." To prove that his father lived a dutiful, virtuous life, the boy read some of his mother's letters to the doctor. As Mrs. Alving softly repeats, "The sins of the fathers!" Oswald confesses of a single instance of "imprudence" that must have infected him. He despairs that he threw his life away for a brief pleasure and asks his mother for something to drink to drown "these gnawing thoughts." Regina brings in a lamp and fetches champagne.

"I can't go on bearing this agony of mind alone," Oswald tells his mother. He would like to take Regina with him and leave home. Because she has "the joy of life in her," Regina will be his salvation. "The joy of life?" asks Mrs. Alving with a start, "Is there salvation in that?" Regina brings more wine and Oswald asks her to fetch a glass for herself. At her mistress' nod, the girl obeys and takes a seat at the table.

Mrs. Alving wants to know more about the "joy of life." People here at home are taught to consider work as a curse and punishment for sin and that life is a state of wretchedness, Oswald explains. No one believes that in Paris, where "the mere fact of being alive is thought to be a matter for exultant happiness. There is light there and sunshine and a holiday feeling," he says. Oswald says he must leave home. If not, "all these feelings that are so strong in me would degenerate into something ugly here," he tells his mother. She regards him steadily for a moment. Now, for the first time, she murmurs, "I see clearly how it all happened. And now I can speak." She is about to tell Oswald and Regina the truth when Manders suddenly enters, cheerful from having spent an "edifying time" at the prayer meeting. He says he has decided that Engstrand needs help with the sailors' home and Regina must go and live with him.

"Regina is going away with me," Oswald states, and Manders turns to Mrs. Alving in bewilderment. "That will not happen either," she declares, and despite the pastor's pleading is about to speak openly. At this moment they hear shouting outside and through the conservatory windows they see a red glare. The orphange is ablaze. "Mrs. Alving, that fire is a judgment on this house of sin!" cries Manders. As they all rush out to the orphange, he is left wringing his hands. "And no insurance," he moans, and then follows them.

Commentary

Formally developing the drama, the second act brings out details and enlarges the action, characterizations and motives which were introduced in the first act. Moreover, the acceleration of events taking place in this scene, their effects heightened by the rich symbolism in Mrs. Alving's "ghosts" speech, leads the audience to await the final nemesis or judgment that will occur in Act III. More specifically, the purpose of this second part is to focus attention on Oswald and complete the characterizations of the secondary characters. By so doing, the playwright can fully disclose the consequences when individuals live by old beliefs and traditional dogma and then assess the guilt for this crime.

Exposing the history of their previous relationship, the conversation between Mrs. Alving and Pastor Manders provides the audience with a completed portrait of the clergyman. First showing Manders' hypocrisy and self-centeredness, Ibsen sums him up as a "big baby." The dramatist, by allowing Engstrand to recite the humbug story of his virtuous life, fully depicts the moral irresponsibility of the carpenter. With these two characters completely developed, Ibsen may now investigate the problem of Mrs. Alving and dwell on the fruits of her cowardice, Regina and Oswald.

Having in common their "joy of life" inherited through their father, Regina and Oswald show their youthful innocence by being unaware of their near-incest relationship. When Mrs. Alving discovers that Oswald, like his father before him, feels that this exuberance of life will degenerate in the sanctimonious home atmosphere, she suddenly understands why her husband became a dissipated drunkard. To prevent further deceit, she prepares Oswald and Regina to comprehend the truth of their origins and the nature of their heritage. As she begins to say the words that will raze these old lies of her past life, they discover the orphanage is ablaze. The symbol of hypocrisy and deceit—a worthy institution to serve society—is destroyed in the moment of truth.

ACT III

Summary

The scene still takes place in Mrs. Alving's home, but it is night time. By now the fire is out, the entire orphanage burned to the ground. While Mrs. Alving has gone to fetch Oswald, Regina and Manders receive Engstrand. "God help us all," he says piously and clucking sympathetically says that the prayer meeting caused the fire. Whispering that "Now we've got the old fool, my girl," he tells Manders, the only one carrying a candle, that he saw the pastor snuff the light and toss the burning wick among the shavings. The distraught reverend is beside himself. The worst aspect of this matter, he says, will be the attacks and slanderous accusations of the newspapers. By this time Mrs. Alving has returned. She considers the fire merely as a business loss; as to the property and the remaining capital in the bank, Manders may use it as he likes. He thinks he may still turn the estate into "some useful community enterprise" and Engstrand is hopeful for his support of the seamen's home. Gloomily, Manders answers that he must first await the published results of the inquiry into the cause of the fire. Offering himself as "an angel of salvation," Engstrand says he will himself answer to the charge. Relieved and breathless, Manders eagerly grasps his hand. "You are one in a thousand," he declares. "You shall have assistance in the matter of your sailors' home, you may rely upon that."

United in friendship, Engstrand and Manders prepare to leave together. Announcing to Mrs. Alving that his enterprise shall be called "The Alving Home," the carpenter concludes, "And if I can carry my own ideas about it, I shall make it worthy of bearing the late Mr. Alving's name." The double entendre is unmistakable to everyone except Manders.

Oswald returns so depressed that Regina is suspicious he may be ill. Mrs. Alving now prepares to tell them both what she started to divulge in the previous scene. What Oswald told her about the joy of life suddenly sheds new light upon everything in her own life, she tells them, for his father, so full of "irrepressible energy and exuberant spirits" in his young days "gave me a holiday feeling just to look at him." Then this boy had to settle in a second-rate town which had none of the joy of life to offer him but only dissipations:

He had to come out here and live an aimless life; he had only an official post. He had no work worth devoting his whole mind to; he had nothing more than official routine to attend to. He had not one single companion capable of appreciating what the joy of life meant; nothing but idlers and tipplers — and so the inevitable happened.

What was the inevitable, asks Oswald, and his mother answers that he had himself described how he would degenerate at home. "Do you mean by that Father — ?" and she nods:

Your poor father never found any outlet for the overmastering joy of life that was in him. And I brought no holiday spirit into his home either. I had been taught about duty and that sort of thing that I believed in so long here. Everything seemed to turn upon duty — my duty or his duty — and I am afraid that I made your poor father's home unbearable to him, Oswald.

Then why did she not write him the truth in her letters, demands the son, and she can only say she never regarded it as something a child should know about. "Your father was a lost man before ever you were born," says Mrs. Alving, and all these years she has kept in mind that Regina "had as good a right in this house — as my own boy had." To their bewilderment she answers quietly, "Yes, now you both know."

"So Mother was one of that sort too," Regina muses. Then she announces her desire to leave them to make good use of her youth before it is wasted. With Oswald sick, she does not wish to spend her life looking after an invalid for "I have the joy of life in me too, Mrs. Alving." From now on she shall make her home in the "Alving Home." Mother and son are alone onstage.

"Let us have a little chat," says Oswald beckoning her to sit beside him. Before he divulges the truth about his fatigue and inability to work he warns her she mustn't scream. The illness itself is hereditary, he continues, and "it lies here (touching his forehead) waiting. At any moment, it may break out." She stifles a cry. At the time he had a serious attack in Paris, Oswald goes on, the doctor told him he would never recover from another one. The disease is a lingering one — the doctor likened it to a "softening of the brain" — and it will leave him hopeless as a vegetable.

Showing his mother a dozen morphia tablets, Oswald says he needed Regina's strength and courage to administer "this last helping hand." Now that Regina is gone, however, his mother must swear that she will give him them herself when it is necessary. Mrs. Alving screams and tries to dash out for the doctor, but Oswald reaches the door first and locks it. "Have you a mother's heart and can bear to see me suffering this unspeakable terror?" he cries out. Trying to control herself, Mrs. Alving trembles violently. "Here is my hand on it," she says.

Outside day is breaking. Oswald is seated quietly in an armchair near the lamp. Cautiously bending over him, Mrs. Alving straightens up, relieved:

It has only been a dreadful fancy of yours, Oswald [she chatters]. ...But now you will get some rest, at home with your own mother, my darling boy...There now, the attack is over. You see how easily it passed off...And look, Oswald, what a lovely day we are going to have. Now you will be able to see your home properly.

She rises and puts out the lamp. In the sunrise the glaciers and peaks in the distance are bathed in bright morning light. Oswald, with his back toward the window, suddenly speaks. "Mother give me the sun." Regarding him with amazement she quavers, "What did you say?" Dully, Oswald repeats, "The sun—the sun." She screams his name. As before, he only says, "The sun—the sun." She beats her head with her hands. "I can't bear it! Never!" she screams. Then, passing her hands over his coat, she searches for the packet of pills. "Where has he got it? Here!" Then she cries, "No, no no!—Yes!—No, no!" Mrs. Alving stares at her son in speechless terror. Oswald remains motionless. "The sun—the sun," he repeats monotonously, and the curtain falls.

Commentary

As in a Greek tragedy, the protagonist's "tragic flaw" involves not only himself, but his children, in the consequences of guilt. In this act Mrs. Alving receives the full penalty for her guilt of substituting a sense of duty for the "joy of life." Her submission to ancient social standards destroys the creative mind of her artist son and similarly destroys Regina's blooming womanhood. The "ghosts" of heredity reappear as Oswald succumbs to syphilitic paresis and as Regina goes to find her future in a brothel. Mrs. Alving can only administer the final stroke — the mortal dose of morphia — to complete the destruction of Oswald she had so unwittingly begun.

With a dramatic flourish, Ibsen uses the environment as an ironic "objective correlative" to underscore the tragedy. As the dawn breaks over a spectacular mountain landscape, Oswald is thrust into the unending darkness of his lingering doom. The long awaited sunshine, so badly needed by Oswald to continue his painting, arrives only to illuminate catastrophe. By the same token, the light of truth has come too late for Mrs. Alving to avoid the consequences of her lifelong deceit.

GENERAL ANALYSIS

THEME

As if to answer the hosts of critics who denounced the "vulgar untruths" they discovered in *A Doll's House,* Ibsen developed another facet of the same idea when he published *Ghosts* two years later. According to Halvdan Koht, one of his biographers, "Mrs. Alving is in reality nothing but a Nora who has tried life and her inherited teachings and who has now taken a stand." Having sacrificed love for conformity, Mrs. Alving must face the tragic consequences of denying her personal needs.

In essence, the problems Ibsen probes in *A Doll's House* are the same as those of *Ghosts:* the relation between past and future, and the relationship between the race and community on one hand, and the individual on the other. Society perpetuates itself by handing down from one generation to another a set of beliefs and customs so that new individuals can take part in the culture and contribute to its perpetuation. Ibsen, however, shows how these principles may degenerate until they actually destroy the very individuals that the social system is created to protect and nurture. He insists that these "ghosts" of old beliefs and outdated piety must be reexamined in the light of each individual's experience; if not, the most gifted of society's children will face destruction.

Having himself suffered all his life under the conservatism of Norwegian provincialism, Ibsen personally found how such a society destroys the "joy of life" in its creative intellects leaving bitterness and frustration.

STRUCTURE AND TECHNIQUE

As in most of Ibsen's problem plays, *Ghosts* begins at the collective climax in the lives of its characters. The play deals only with the consequences of these past lives and does not need to take place in more than one twenty-four hour vigil. Although the relationships among the characters are close and lifelong, only the crowding of emotions and events within these three acts forces each one to face the truth about himself and about his society.

Unlike *A Doll's House,* where there are servants and a sub-plot between Krogstad and Mrs. Linde, only five characters appear in *Ghosts.* No one is included who has not a place in the main action itself. In this way, an atmosphere of austere grandeur is given to the whole drama providing it with an intensity suggestive of classical plays. Professor Koht describes the play's further relationship to ancient drama for Greek tragedy, often called the fate, or family drama, shows a tragic flaw inherited through the generations. *Ghosts* is also a "family tragedy," he writes, "but it is also a social drama — the ancient tragedy resurrected on modern soil."

Captain Alving's character bears this out. The source of the hereditary flaw which destroys his children, his presence pervades each scene of *Ghosts.* As each living character illuminates the nature of the diseased profligate, he finally stands as clearly and as well-drawn to the audience as if he were constantly active on stage. Almost as a "secondary" protagonist, Alving undergoes a change of character until he is presented to the spectator as an individual whom society has wronged. Finally, when Mrs. Alving recognizes how she destroyed his "joy of life," the dead husband is no longer a ghost, but a humanized victim of the social conventions.

CHARACTER ANALYSIS

Pastor Manders

Pastor Manders, simple-minded and self-involved like Torvald Helmer, exists in an imaginary world where people and events conform to his stereotypes. Depositions such as "It is not a wife's part to be her husband's judge" and "We have no right to do anything that will scandalize the community" show how he accepts all the verbal expressions of social principles but is unable to deal with instances where doctrine does not apply. When he states, for instance, "A child should love and honor his father and mother," Mrs. Alving tartly replies, "Don't let us talk in such general terms. Suppose we say: ought Oswald to love and honor Mr. Alving?" To this conflict of principle and reality which she suggests, the reverend has no response. Hypocritical and prideful, Manders' only reaction to the story of Joanna's scandalous marriage to Engstrand is indignation that he was fooled.

Because of the power that his clerical status accords him, Manders is the most destructive creature in the drama. Incapable of spontaneity, devoid of any intellect, he readily sacrifices individual integrity and freedom of expression to maintain empty social standards. The major incident in a life devoted to hypocrisy occurred when Manders persuaded Mrs. Alving to return to her husband. Delighted to show the world his victory over temptation, he neglected Mrs. Alving's plight. His indifference to the needs of the individual sacrificed the love of a sensitive young woman and doomed her to lifelong despair. Although he is a believable figure in the present play, Manders is too much a stereotype. He speaks for all of society and represents its evils.

Mrs. Alving

Mrs. Alving, raised as a dutiful girl to become a dutiful wife and mother, would easily fall in love with the virtuous Manders. Certainly a man with Alving's exuberance and vitality would not be a suitable husband for her. However, desperate circumstances forced Mrs. Alving to reassess the values she was brought up to maintain. Suffering her hard life with Alving, taking over his business, reading and thinking for herself revitalized her static intellect. By the end of the play she is able to recognize that her sanctimoniousness contributed to perverting Alving's joy of life into lechery and drunkenness. This final awakening comes too late: the ghosts of her past education have already destroyed the children in her care, Regina and Oswald.

What makes Mrs. Alving such an interesting character is her inability to take a stand between keeping up appearances and acting out of personal integrity. At the same time she reads controversial literature and regrets the deceit in her past life, she dedicates a town orphanage to preserve the reputation of her dead husband. Although encouraging Oswald to study art and educating Regina to be a gentlewoman, she raises her son to idealize his father and never tells Regina the facts of her origins. No longer deceiving herself as to the truth of Manders' pious generalizations, Mrs. Alving instills these same "ghosts" into the beliefs of her children.

In another sense, the personal tension in Mrs. Alving is based on her imposed feminine weaknesses in a society where only men expect to express themselves aggressively and self-confidently. In this way, Ibsen recalls the feminist sympathy he expressed in *A Doll's House*, and depicts another tragedy where a woman finally asserts her own individuality and intellect after catastrophe.

Oswald Alving

Oswald Alving, although important in the play, is merely a minor character and represents the doomed product of a diseased society. Artistically gifted by having inherited his father's "joy of life," he finds he cannot work at home where the "sun" of self-expression is obscured by the "fog" of duty and social appearances. Fearing that his exuberance and creativity would dissipate, like that of his father, under these circumstances, he wants to leave home with Regina. However Oswald is doomed by a more drastic form of hereditary dissipation; he ends his life in hopeless lunacy, crying vainly for the sun—the symbolic sun of truth, love, and self-expression that he never found among his own people.

Regina

Regina Engstrand is another victim of society's "ghosts" which destroy the "joy of life" in its female members. Limited by her sex and status, she is unable to channel this vitality into a constructive mode of life. Unable to marry into another social level, Regina has no resources with which to face her future other than her own good looks and spirited temperament.

Jacob Engstrand

Jacob Engstrand, made cynical by his experiences as a member of the lower class, preys upon the established society for his maintenance. Using the same tools of hypocrisy and deceit that Pastor Manders accepts as social principles, Engstrand gains in power and prestige. He personifies how Manders' pious idealism degenerates into ruthless self-interest when social principles are applied to denounce individual integrity.

SYMBOLISM

Ibsen's poetic ability enables him to enrich the prose plays with symbols that have broad as well as narrow meanings. Especially allusive is Ibsen's concept of light and darkness. Oswald's last plea for the sun, for instance, sums up his need for the "joy of life" in himself as well as in his work. He needs sunlight in which to paint and he needs illumination on the nature of his father. A pall hangs over the entire landscape of the play; if there is no rain at the moment, the scene outside the window is obscured by mist. The weather finally clears when Mrs. Alving faces the truth, but it is too late. Thrust into darkness, Oswald weakly cries out for the sun. His last monosyllabic plea has a twofold significance: not only symbolizing the "light of truth," it might stand for the morphia powders which would dispel the lingering darkness that enshrouds Oswald's diseased mind.

The fire that destroys the orphange is another symbol of truth. Purifying the institution of deceit, the flames allow Engstrand to receive support for his planned Alving Home. With characteristic irony, Ibsen implies that there is no deceit in raising a brothel to the memory of the late Captain Alving.

The most pervasive symbol, of course, is that of ghosts. The ghosts are worn ideals and principles of law and order so misapplied that they have no actual significance. All the untested maxims and abstract dogma that Manders maintains are ghosts; all the sources of personal cowardice in Mrs. Alving are ghosts. Ghosts are also the lies about the past, perpetrated to the present, which will haunt the future. Finally, ghosts are the actual and symbolic diseases of heredity which destroy the joy of life in the younger, freer generations.

AN ENEMY OF THE PEOPLE

ACT I

Summary

In the home of Dr. Stockmann, Mrs. Stockmann is offering Mr. Billings, an assistant on the local paper, some more food. She thinks she hears the editor, Mr. Hovstad coming, but it is her brother-in-law, the Mayor (or Burgomaster). He is somewhat shocked to see that the Stockmanns have meat for supper. Mr. Hovstad appears and tells the Burgomaster that he is here on business. Dr. Stockmann often writes an article for Mr. Hovstad's liberal paper. The present article Dr. Stockmann is having printed is about the medicinal value of the new baths which are soon to open up in the town. The Burgomaster speaks about the great value of the baths to the town, but he resents the idea that his brother is credited with being the founder of the baths because he himself was responsible for the execution of the plan.

Dr. Stockmann comes in bringing with him another guest, an old friend named Captain Horster. He greets his brother and explains how great it is now to have a job where he can afford to eat meat twice a day and to buy little items. For many years, he has had to live on almost starvation wages, but now that the Burgomaster has gotten him a position with the baths, he is always in good spirits. The Burgomaster wants to know about the new article Dr. Stockmann is publishing, but Dr. Stockmann tells him it isn't to appear until he checks on a few more facts. The Burgomaster knows that the article is about the baths and demands to be told immediately all about it. When Dr. Stockmann refuses, the Burgomaster leaves in anger.

Hovstad comes in and intimates that the Burgomaster left because the crowd was too liberal for him. There is a town election coming soon and Hovstad's liberal paper has not been supporting the Burgomaster. Petra Stockmann comes in from the school where she teaches and tells her father that she has a letter for him. Dr. Stockmann becomes excited and goes immediately to his study to read the letter. His wife explains to the guests that Dr. Stockmann has been waiting every day for a week for some mysterious letter.

Petra tells the group how difficult it is to teach when the little children have to be told so many things that are not true. She would like to open a school of her own. Captain Horster offers her the bottom of his old house which stands empty most of the time, especially since he is about to sail for America. Hovstad thinks she would do better to come over to journalism and asks her if she has finished the translation of the English novel. She promises to have it completed in a short time.

Dr. Stockmann comes back in and is excited about the news he has just received. He thinks he has made a great discovery. He tells them that he has found out that their magnificent, lovely, highly praised baths are nothing more than a poisonous, pestiferous hole. He explains that the pipes are laid too low and all the filth from the tanning mills is infecting the water. He has spent the entire winter investigating the affair and has sent off samples of the water to the university for analysis. The water contains millions of putrefying organic matter called infusoria. These are detrimental to health whether they are used internally or externally. He explains that this was why so many people were sick last summer at the baths. At the time he thought the people brought the disease with them, but now he knows that they became sick from the water. To correct the situation, all of the water pipes will have to be relaid.

Dr. Stockmann explains that the town has often laughed at his ideas and proposals, but now everyone will see that he is not out of his head. He particularly wants Petra to tell her grandfather who has thought Dr. Stockmann was "not quite right." Furthermore, he has prepared a statement for the directors of the baths and is going to send it to the Burgomaster immediately. Hovstad wants to put a short announcement of the discovery in the paper, and it is suggested that the town should do something to honor Dr. Stockmann. Dr. Stockmann thinks, however, that it is a blessing to have served his native town and its citizens.

Commentary

The first act is concerned with providing background information and other matters of exposition. We are not far enough in the play yet to draw definite character personalities. The exposition (i.e., the handling of background material) provides us with the knowledge that Dr. Stockmann has often been on the verge of extreme poverty, that his brother the Burgomaster has obtained a nice post for him with the new baths in the town, that the idea of the baths were originally Dr. Stockmann's, but the Burgomaster took over and directed the building of the baths along lines which Dr. Stockmann did not approve of. Furthermore, we find out that the two brothers have very little in common. The Burgomaster adheres to old and traditional views and Dr. Stockmann is a man of modern and liberal views. At this point, it is suggested that Hovstad is in agreement with Dr. Stockmann and opposed to the Burgomaster, but this will later be dramatically reversed.

There are also enough hints in this first act to indicate that Dr. Stockmann is an impulsive man. He writes articles for the newspaper on any new idea he has. He does things impetuously and without consultation. He has had many "crackbrained notions" in the past, and has refused to consult the proper authorities.

Dr. Stockmann is also somewhat naive in thinking that the community will be proud of him for discovering that the baths are poisonous. He fails to realize that as important as the discovery is, it is one which will cause an immense amount of expense and inconvenience. Furthermore, there seems to be some ambiguity in his motivations. We know that he was annoyed at the Burgomaster for refusing to lay the pipes where Dr. Stockmann wanted them. Now that he has found out that the pipes are causing the baths to be poisonous, there is a hint of personal satisfaction in proving the Burgomaster wrong. In fact, his happiness can derive directly from his vindication against the Burgomaster who refused to follow Dr. Stockmann's specification for building the baths.

In the statement that Dr. Stockmann has prepared, the reader must inquire whether this statement is an explanation or an accusation. Dr. Stockmann is somewhat naive and innocent when he thinks that the Burgomaster will be pleased at this discovery.

The act ends on a note of irony. Dr. Stockmann thinks that he is going to be honored as a hero and feels good that he served his town and fellow citizens well. It will be only a short time before he will be declared an enemy of the people.

At the end of the first act, the problem has not yet been fully presented. Now it is only that the baths are unsanitary and the conditions of the baths must be changed or altered.

ACT II

Summary
Dr. Stockmann has his manuscript returned to him with a note from the Burgomaster that they should meet at noontime. Mrs. Stockmann suggests that perhaps he should share the honor with his brother. Dr. Stockmann is willing to share the honor if he can get the thing straightened out.

Old Morton Kiil, the man who adopted and raised Mrs. Stockmann, drops by to inquire if the news is correct. He thinks it is a good trick to play on the Burgomaster. Dr. Stockmann doesn't understand. Morton Kiil asks if these poisonous animals are invisible and then says that the Burgomaster will never fall for such a story as that. But he is angry with the Burgomaster and the town council and hopes that his son-in-law will make them all "eat humble pie." When Hovstad drops by, Morton Kiil wonders if Hovstad is also involved. Now he is convinced that Stockmann and Hovstad are in some conspiracy to make the Burgomaster look foolish.

When old Morton Kiil leaves, Dr. Stockmann is astounded at the possibility that people won't believe him. Hovstad points out that a good many other things are involved aside from the medical aspect. He suggests that the poison comes not just from the tanning mills, but also from the poisonous life that the entire community is living. The "town has gradually drifted into the hands of a pack of bureaucrats," and that is why the pipes were laid in the wrong place to begin with. The leaders of the town show no foresight and no ability. He wants to take up the matter in the paper and use the case of the baths to clear the town council of all the "obstinate old blockheads" who are holding progress back. This is their chance to "emancipate the downtrodden masses."

Aslaksen, the printer, appears and offers his support to Dr. Stockmann. He is the head of the "compact majority in the town" and is sure the compact majority will stand behind Dr. Stockmann. He is thinking of some type of demonstration if one could be held with moderation. Dr. Stockmann explains that he needs no support because the issues are so clear and self-evident. But Aslaksen reminds him that the authorities always move slowly.

After Aslaksen leaves, Hovstad insists that "this gross, inexcusable blunder of the water-works must be brought home clearly to every voter." Dr. Stockmann asks him to wait until he can consult with his brother. After Hovstad leaves, Dr. Stockmann tells his family how good it feels to be able to do something good for his town.

The Burgomaster comes in to discuss the baths with Dr. Stockmann. He asks Dr. Stockmann if he checked to see how much new pipes would cost and how long it would take. They would cost around sixty thousand dollars and would take two years to relay. In the meantime, the baths would have to be closed down and after word got around that they were poisonous, no one would ever come to them anymore and the town would be literally bankrupt. He tells Dr. Stockmann that his report will literally ruin the town and that Dr. Stockmann will be responsible for the total destruction of his own town. Dr. Stockmann is shocked, but says that the baths are still contaminated and something must be done. The Burgomaster, however, is not convinced that the condition is as serious as Dr.

Stockmann says it is. He accuses his brother of exaggerating great-ly, and suggests that a competent physician should be able to do something to rectify the situation. But Dr. Stockmann asserts that anything short of relaying the pipes would be dishonest: it would be "a fraud, a lie, an absolute crime against the public, against society as a whole." He believes it is just stubbornness and fear of blame that keeps the Burgomaster from recognizing the disastrous state of the baths. Dr. Stockmann reminds the Burgomaster that the plan of the baths was "bungled" by the authorities, and now these same people cannot admit they were wrong. The Burgomaster reminds Dr. Stockmann that as an individual he has no right to an individual opinion and must always rely on the authorities. He therefore for-bids Dr. Stockmann to turn in his report or to meddle any further in the affairs of the baths. Furthermore, he demands that Dr. Stockmann obey him. But the doctor says he will take his case to the papers and will write against the Burgomaster: he will prove that the "source is poisoned" and that the people "live by trafficking in filth and cor-ruption. The whole of our flourishing social life is rooted in a lie."

The Burgomaster warns Dr. Stockmann that such "offensive insinuations against his native place" will brand him as an enemy of society. After the Burgomaster leaves, Dr. Stockmann is proud to know that he has the independent press and the compact majority behind him. He is determined to carry out his plan. Mrs. Stockmann reminds him that he has a family to look after and they might suffer dire consequences. Dr. Stockmann, however, feels that he must stand by his principles or he would never "have the right to look my boys in the face."

Commentary

Act I only presented the need of the baths to be cleansed. Act II begins to develop the problem with more implications. We are now able to see that the play is going to handle the broad subject of *private* vs. *public* morality. Or as the problem will later be de-veloped, the conflict between *personal integrity* and *social obliga-tion*. This idea will be more fully developed in later acts.

This act presents our first hint of the public's refusal to believe Stockmann. It comes from Stockmann's father-in-law. He believes that Dr. Stockmann is slyly trying to avenge himself against his brother by making the Burgomaster and the entire town council admit that they made a tremendous mistake. If Dr. Stockmann can do that, old Morton Kiil will be happy because they had previously forced him off the town council.

With the appearance of Hovstad, we see the liberal who is ready to jump at any cause and champion that cause as long as he thinks the cause will be popular and will increase circulation.

With Aslaksen, we see the man of cautious good will. He wants to do everything with moderation and not offend anyone. He represents the "compact majority" – that group of people who have no opinions and who follow others like a herd of animals.

When the Burgomaster appears, Dr. Stockmann is shocked to find out that his proposal will cost so much and will take so long to effect. The Burgomaster then is seen as a practical man who believes that the men in authority should decide everything. His view is that the individual freedom should be subjected to the demands of the authorities. This is, of course, a legitimate view, but Ibsen does not leave it a clash between two opposing ideological views. The Burgomaster's views must be seen in terms of his personal involvement. If the news of the baths is made public, he as the authority will be seen to have made a mistake. This will be a personal slight. But also, if the news of the baths is made public, the town will suffer tremendous losses and will be virtually destroyed; thus, his duty as the chief magistrate of the town is to try to save the town. Thus as was Dr. Stockmann's discovery tainted by his desire to avenge himself against the authorities, so now is the Burgomaster's defense somewhat tinged with personal motives.

Dr. Stockmann is still seen as somewhat the impractical visionary. He can see nothing except that the baths are dangerous and poisonous. It may be suggested that he is so confident in his views since he knows (or thinks) that the press and the compact majority are behind him. And under all circumstances, he is a man who does believe strongly in personal freedom and will not submit blindly to the rule of the authorities.

Mrs. Stockmann is seen in this scene as the eternal matriarch; that is, she is the eternal mother and wife figure whose main concern is with the personal welfare of her immediate family.

At the end of the act, we find that perhaps the town will consider Dr. Stockmann an enemy of the society. This is, of course, ironic because Dr. Stockmann thought he was doing a great service to the community. It is his desire to serve his fellow man that hurts more than anything else. Unlike the Burgomaster who believes that the people are like a herd and not worthy of consideration, Dr. Stockmann here believes in the potential capabilities of all the people and counts strongly on the general public to see his point of view.

ACT III

Summary
In the editor's room of the "People's Messenger," Hovstad and his assistant, Billing, are discussing Dr. Stockmann's article. They feel that now the Burgomaster is in trouble and they will use this trouble to hound him out of office. They hope to replace him with men of more "liberal ideas."

Dr. Stockmann arrives and tells the men to go ahead with the publication of his article. They call Aslaksen who wants to know if the article will offend people. He is assured that all intelligent and prudent men will support the article. Dr. Stockmann believes that his article will send all the old bunglers packing, and the town will have a new regime. Aslaksen insists that they proceed with moderation. He explains that he has learned caution when attacking local authorities. If it is a subject of attacking the national government, he is not timid, but with local authorities, one must proceed with caution. Billing maintains that Dr. Stockmann will be declared "a Friend of the People."

After Dr. Stockmann and Aslaksen leave, Hovstad wishes that they could get some financial backing from someone else so that they wouldn't have to rely on Aslaksen. They think about old Morton Kiil who is bound to have some money and the money will go to Dr. Stockmann's family. At this time, Petra comes in to explain that she refuses to translate a certain English novel because it does not conform with Hovstad's liberal ideas. The novel is unrealistic and false to life. Hovstad explains that the paper must print something to attract the attention of the reader so as to trap him into reading the more important liberal ideas. Petra feels this is not honorable and is somewhat disgusted. In further discussions, Petra sees that Hovstad is "not the man" he pretended to be, and she tells him that she will never trust him again.

As Petra leaves, Aslaksen comes in to tell Hovstad that the Burgomaster is in the printing office. After some small talk, the Burgomaster sees Dr. Stockmann's article. He wants to know if the paper is going to print and support Dr. Stockmann's position. He inquires about the compact majority and pretends to be surprised that so many of the "poorer class appear to be so heroically eager to make sacrifices." Aslaksen and Hovstad are confused. The Burgomaster explains that it will require this huge sum of money, which will have to come from the town, and the project will take two years to complete. In the meantime, other towns will take over the business and when the news reaches other places, no one will ever come to their town. Hovstad and Aslaksen now see that Dr. Stockmann was not informed of all the facts. The Burgomaster explains that he is not convinced that there is anything wrong with the water supply. He has brought with him a short statement of what should be done about the baths and wonders if the paper will care to print it.

Just as Hovstad is accepting the paper, they see Dr. Stockmann approaching. The Burgomaster hides in the next room. Dr. Stockmann asks if the first proofs on his article are ready. He is told it will be quite some time. He warns his friends not to get up any type of testimonial for him because it would be too embarrassing. Mrs. Stockmann comes in and warns her husband of the trouble he is getting the entire family into. At this time, Dr. Stockmann notices the Burgomaster's hat and cane. He routs his brother out of hiding and tells him that the power has now changed hands. But Aslaksen and Hovstad take the Burgomaster's side. Both explain that Dr. Stockmann's plan will ruin the town. Dr. Stockmann refuses to budge from his position. He maintains that the truth cannot be killed by a "conspiracy of silence." He promises that his report will be made public in spite of all threats. As the men turn against Dr. Stockmann, his wife comes to his side and promises to stand by him always. He is told he can have no hall to speak in and no society will listen to him. He threatens to stand on the street corner and read his paper to the people.

Commentary

Act III is the changing point in the drama. Here we see the various motives of the characters examined under pressures and thus we find out who are the real men of principles. At the first of the act when Aslaksen and Hovstad think that the doctor's discovery will be popular and beneficial and when they think it will provide an opportunity to get rid of the old authorities, they are supporting him. Later when they realize that it will be harmful to the town and therefore unpopular, they turn against the doctor. Aslaksen is a man who does not wish to offend anyone and who wants to proceed with moderation. But more important, when his principles are confronted with the possibility that he will lose financially, the principles are no longer important.

With Hovstad, we see in his discussion with Petra, that he is not a man of true principles. He publishes not what he believes in but what he thinks will increase circulation. Thus his allegiance to Dr. Stockmann stems not from a belief in the truth of Dr. Stockmann's ideas, but from the hope that his cause will be a popular one and thus increase circulation.

With the appearance of the Burgomaster, the theme of personal integrity and social obligation becomes dominant. The Burgomaster is attempting to save the town, but in doing so, he is also trying to preserve his image as the town's foremost citizen. If the report is made public, it will destroy both the town and the Burgomaster's reputation because he was responsible for the construction of the water pipes which cause all the trouble. Thus for the benefit of the town and his own personal integrity, he refuses to believe the truth of Dr. Stockmann's report and hints that the doctor has always been impetuous and wild in his ideas.

Dr. Stockmann is now seen as the impractical idealist. In striving to achieve the ideal or the perfectly moral solution, he ignores all practical advice and opposes everyone who would stand in his way. In other words, he is ready to carry his idealism to absurd degrees.

Mrs. Stockmann is somewhat comic in these scenes. She is opposed to her husband's plans until the people turn against him. Then she is ready to stand by him simply because he is her husband. She doesn't understand what is at stake here, but is nevertheless convinced that her husband is right even though a few moments earlier she was trying to get him to change.

ACT IV

Summary

In the large bottom room of Captain Horster's house, there is to be a meeting. It is heard that Dr. Stockmann was unable to find another meeting place and his old friend offered him this place. The citizens gathering are wondering what they should do. They decide to watch Aslaksen and do as he does. Dr. Stockmann and his family arrive and the Burgomaster comes in from another direction. Hovstad and Billing are also there.

Before Dr. Stockmann can start his speech, the Burgomaster and Aslaksen insist that a chairman be elected. Dr. Stockmann points out that it is unnecessary since he only wants to give a lecture. But a chairman is elected. It is Aslaksen. Then the Burgomaster moves that the meeting decline to hear the lecture on the subject of the baths. After more speeches and confusion, Dr. Stockmann tells the audience that he does not wish to speak on the subject of the baths but on something entirely different. He is allowed to begin.

The theme of Dr. Stockmann's speech is that the "sources of our spiritual life are poisoned, and that our whole society rests upon a pestilential basis of falsehood." He then attacks the leading men who act like goats and do harm at every point. They block the path of a free man and are filled with prejudices. But more dangerous is the compact majority. The country should be run by the intelligent men and since the majority is made up of fools, it should have no right to a voice in the government. He proves that with animals only the thoroughbreds are worth anything. The same should be true with people. The herd of men are no better than curs, and should be kept in that position.

At this point the crowd begins to revolt. A motion is made to declare Dr. Stockmann an enemy of the people. The motion is passed with only one person voting against it. Old Morton Kiil comes to Stockmann and wonders if the poison comes from his tannery as well as the others. Dr. Stockmann tells him that the Morton Kiil Tannery is one of the worst and will have to be improved immediately. Old Morton Kiil tells Stockmann that such an accusation may cost the Stockmann family a lot of money.

Dr. Stockmann asks Captain Horster if he has room on his ship for the Stockmanns to sail with him to America. Captain Horster tells him that he will make room.

Commentary
The act opens with Stockmann still convinced that he is working for the sake of the people. Thinking that he will now become the champion of the people, he obtains a hall in order to give a lecture. Thus, this act pits the idealist against the common herd of people, the people whom Stockmann wants to serve.

Apparently, Stockmann wanted to give his speech about the baths. But the democratic principles of electing a chairman for the committee and then entertaining a motion as to whether Dr. Stockmann should be heard changed the nature of the speech. He therefore delivers a tirade against the democratic processes and attempts to prove that the common man has no business having a voice in the government. He is, of course, still the idealist, but here the idealist is trapped in the involved processes of bureaucracy. He sees his idealism being defeated by the very people he wanted to help; thus, he attacks the people and the officials elected by the officials.

The reader must realize that Stockmann's speech is offensive. But he remains a sympathetic character because the purpose of his speech is noble. He is striving to realize his ideals without compromising his principles. Everyone else at the meeting has in one way or another compromised himself — has sold out for personal gain or to avoid a difficult conflict. But in his attack, we must step back and realize that Dr. Stockmann has carried idealism to its extreme.

The question arises then: Is Dr. Stockmann an enemy of the people? If we were to isolate Dr. Stockmann's speech, that is, take it out of the context of all that went before, and if we were to hear only what the audience at Dr. Stockmann's speech heard, then we would see that Dr. Stockmann's present position is one that justifies his being called an enemy of the people. He has openly advocated that the people are not capable of voting correctly. He has insulted the common people and has referred to them in terms of a herd of animals. Thus, by this speech alone, Dr. Stockmann is an enemy of the people. But actually, we know that his attack is motivated by more noble reasons and only in his disillusionment does he make such heavy charges against the very people he wants to help.

ACT V

Summary
Dr. Stockmann's home is in disorder. He appears holding a stone which someone cast through his window. He wants to save it as a reminder of his days of persecution. He receives a letter from the landlord giving him notice to move. Petra arrives from the school and tells her family that she has been dismissed. All of this is because the people are afraid to go against the popular opinion. Captain Horster comes in and tells them that he has lost his ship because the owner is afraid of popular opinion. Next the Burgomaster arrives and hands Dr. Stockmann his dismissal from the baths. The Burgomaster tells Dr. Stockmann that a circular is being sent around advising people not to engage Dr. Stockmann. He suggests to Dr. Stockmann that he could be reinstated in a couple of months if he would write a document saying that all of his ideas about the baths were false. But Dr. Stockmann refuses.

The Burgomaster accuses Doctor Stockmann of acting so highly because he knows of old Morton Kiil's will. But Dr. Stockmann knows nothing. The Burgomaster tells him that old Morton Kiil is wealthy and is leaving a large portion of his fortune to Dr. Stockmann's children and that he and Mrs. Stockmann are to have the "life-interest" on it. Dr. Stockmann is tremendously relieved to know that his wife and children are taken care of. The Burgomaster accuses Dr. Stockmann of creating all the trouble simply because Old Morton Kiil has a quarrel with the town council. Dr. Stockmann is almost speechless and calls his wife to scrub the floor where the Burgomaster walked out.

Shortly, Old Morton Kiil comes to call upon Dr. Stockmann. He explains that he has been out buying up shares of the baths with the money which he was to leave Mrs. Stockmann and the children. He feels that his tannery is the cause of the foulness in the water and he wants Stockmann to clear the Morton Kiil name. Thus, if Dr. Stockmann continues in his insistence upon the destructive element involved in the baths, then he is cutting off his own family from a large inheritance. Dr. Stockmann is stunned, and says he will talk to his wife. After all, the people have turned against him and he can do very little. He is to let Morton Kiil know by two o'clock.

As Morton Kiil is leaving, Hovstad and Aslaksen arrive. They immediately ask Dr. Stockmann if his father-in-law hasn't been buying stocks in the baths. Then they suggest it would have been more prudent of Dr. Stockmann to have let them in on his little plan of secretly buying up the baths stocks after giving out the false rumors. This is too much for Dr. Stockmann. He grabs his stick and drives both men out of the house. He calls Petra and sends his answer immediately to Old Morton Kiil. He then tells his wife that they will stay in the town and fight all the worse elements. He will found a school and teach the street curs how to think and act properly. He has, he says, learned one great lesson—the strongest man is the man who stands alone.

Commentary
     Act V is a practical or materialistic test of Dr. Stockmann's idealism. In the last act, we saw Aslaksen and Hovstad retract when they stood to lose something personally. This act now confronts Dr.

Stockmann with great personal losses if he continues to assert his views. This test is necessary before we can formulate a complete view of Dr. Stockmann.

Before he faces his test, he first learns that his views have caused Captain Horster to lose his ship and Petra to lose her position in the school. Furthermore he has faced his own dismissal from the baths. Thus when Old Morton Kiil comes to him asking him to retract his charges or else all of his inheritance will go to charity, Dr. Stockmann is about ready to yield to the public opinion. He is prevented by the appearance of Hovstad and Aslaksen. When Dr. Stockmann sees that he can gain the admiration of his fellow townsmen by admitting that he engineered the entire plan so as to gain control of the stock of the baths, this accusation (or this admiration) is worse than the rejection by the people. He therefore decides to stand by his idealistic views.

Finally we must note that Dr. Stockmann's idealism is not consistent. In Act IV he denied that the common curs could be of any value to society. But in Act V, he says he is going to take the common "street-curs" and educate them into the leading men of society who will then drive out all the bureaucrats. His saving factor, however, is his strong belief in that which is right.

GENERAL ANALYSIS

STRUCTURE AND TECHNIQUE

As with most problem plays, *An Enemy of the People* takes a specific situation and uses it to make a larger general statement about mankind. Here we have the specific problem of the bad water pipes at the new health baths. The question then is simply one of cleaning the baths. It is a matter of civic health and sanitation. From this specific situation, Ibsen then moves to the more complex problem of private versus public morality. Or to state it in other words, Ibsen is investigating the relationship between moral and ethical responsibility when seen against practical exigency.

To present this problem, Ibsen creates an idealist in the person of Dr. Stockmann and has him diametrically opposed by his own brother who is the man of extreme practicality. In other words, Dr. Stockmann represents private and public morality while his brother, the Burgomaster, represents the practical aspect of life.

The problem which perplexes many readers of this play is Ibsen's apparent failure to make his position clear. But this was not Ibsen's purpose. He is not offering a stated solution to his problem, but instead, he is presenting a full measured discussion of the problem. The sensible man would assume a position somewhere between that of Dr. Stockmann and the Burgomaster. In his idealism, Dr. Stockmann forgets that the world moves by practical means. It is revealed early in the play that Dr. Stockmann conceived the idea of the baths but could never bring them to a practical completion. It took the Burgomaster to do that. Thus, Dr. Stockmann is seen essentially as a comic figure whose idealism blinds him to the commonplace practicality of the world. But the Burgomaster is equally as blinded to the ethical questions of the world. Therefore, after a thorough consideration of the ideas, the reader should take a stand somewhere between the two extremes represented by the main characters.

CHARACTER ANALYSIS

Aslaksen

Aslaksen is the man of cautious good will. His constant comment involves "proceeding with moderation." He is afraid of offending anyone who is in authority, unless that person is some distant abstract person who cannot immediately affect him. He represents the compact majority who believes in civic progress so long as it does not involve any expense or effort. He is the type who would rather suffer any type of bad situation rather than get involved in a drastic change.

Hovstad

Hovstad is the professional type of liberal who constantly wants to stir things up as long as he is not directly involved and will not be personally affected. His main concern is to increase the circulation of his paper, and for this purpose he will ignore any principle.

48

He supports Dr. Stockmann as long as he thinks the compact majority and the public are behind Dr. Stockmann. But as soon as it is known that the public will not support any idea which is going to cost money, he turns against Dr. Stockmann and supports the Burgomaster.

Mrs. Stockmann

She is a minor character who represents the eternal matriarch. Her interest is in the family. She does not care for civic causes, but when her husband is attacked by other people, she comes to his side even though she does not understand the principles behind the cause.

Peter Stockmann, (The Burgomaster)

The Burgomaster represents the old established order of things. He believes that authority should rest in the hands of the officials and that all individuals should be subjected to the rule of these authorities. He does not believe in personal or individual expressions. He is convinced that he is right and anyone opposed to him must be wrong. He tells Dr. Stockmann that "the individual must subordinate himself to society, or, more precisely, to the authorities whose business it is to watch over the welfare of society." He is, then, the reactionary who is afraid of any change because change implies a reevaluation of authority.

The Burgomaster is not a man of strong ethical principles. Instead, he is the practical man who looks to see how something will bring a practical or material reward. He cannot conceive of the possibility that he might be wrong in anything. Thus part of his opposition to Dr. Stockmann's news about the baths is due to the fact that the Burgomaster was responsible for placing the water-pipes in the wrong place. He is incapable of facing the fact that he made a tremendous error, and therefore, he must repress the news of the bad sanitary conditions so that his own reputation will be preserved.

Dr. Stockmann

Dr. Stockmann represents the extreme idealist who has no concept of the practical side of life. His idealism blinds him to the common procedures of everyday activity.

As an idealist, Dr. Stockmann believes strongly in individual freedom and the right of every man to express himself freely. He cannot become a party to any dishonest or unethical act. Thus, he cannot bend in any sense of the word. He is accurately characterized as too impetuous. As soon as he finds out about the bad sanitary conditions at the baths, he immediately makes the news public and refuses to listen to any compromise and demands that the water pipes be relaid. He does not try to convince the people of his view, but instead, goes directly and blindly at a demanded improvement. It is, therefore, his lack of tact and understanding of the practical issues which place him in such an awkward position.

There is, however, a touch of jealous revenge in Dr. Stockmann's actions. He was annoyed that the Burgomaster did not build the pipes according to the doctor's original specifications, and thus he is delighted that he is able to prove the Burgomaster to be wrong.

Furthermore, Dr. Stockmann's idealism is somewhat muddled. He is not consistent. At one point he maintains that the common people have no right to a voice in the government. But this is what the Burgomaster had previously told the doctor and the doctor had stoutly asserted the right of every citizen to express his own views. Likewise, he suggests that the common people are like curs or impure animals and can never be educated to take a significant role in the development of a society. Yet at the end he is going to take some "street-curs" and educate them to run the wolves out of the government.

Dr. Stockmann is saved as a character because he puts his principles above his own desires and gains. He is not tempted by financial rewards enough to deny the truth of the condition of the baths. He is thoroughly disgusted by the petty and dishonest interpretations placed on his actions. And as a man of great personal integrity, he spurns a large inheritance in order to maintain an ethical and moral responsibility to himself and to his community.

THE WILD DUCK

INTRODUCTION

As in previous plays, Ibsen uses his "retrospective technique" which, in the words of George Brandes, a contemporary critic, "is the principle of advancing by going backwards to the revelations of the past." The characters in *The Wild Duck* are related through complicated events in their past history, and, for the sake of efficiency, these relationships are outlined under "Character Analysis."

ACT I

Summary

Mr. Werle is giving a party in honor of his son's homecoming. Besides influential political friends, he has also invited Hialmar Ekdal, an old schoolfellow of Gregers. Feeling out of place and uncomfortable among the guests, Hialmar is more gloomy than ever when he overhears Werle whisper to Gregers that he hopes none noticed that they were thirteen at table. His friend however reassures him; feeling more alien in his father's house than Hialmar feels, Gregers avers that he himself is "the thirteenth."

In another room, the servants reluctantly admit Old Ekdal. He explains that he has come to fetch some copy work which the bookkeeper left for him, and, unseen by the guests, he steals into the office.

Conversing with his old friend, Gregers is surprised to learn that Hialmar has married their former maidservant. Gina is a different person than the one he knew as a servant, young Ekdal explains; "she is by no means without culture" for "life itself is an education." He boasts that "her daily intercourse with me" has refined her "and then we know one or two rather remarkable men who come a good deal about us."

Thronging into the room, the chamberlains are joking with Mrs. Sorby who keeps up the witty repartee. Gregers advises his friend to join the conversation, but Hialmar does not know what to say. During a discussion about wines, he makes the guests laugh by asking whether vintages differ according to their seasons. As Werle involuntarily exclaims "Ugh," the guests turn to see the shabbily dressed Lieutenant Ekdal walk with the bookkeeper to the front door. Hialmar turns his back and faces the fireplace. When asked whether he knew that man, the son stammers "I don't know—I didn't notice" while Gregers recovers from his shock at old Ekdal's appearance. Reproaching Hialmar, young Werle says, "And you could stand there and deny that you knew him!" but the loudness of the guests interrupts their further conversation.

When Werle has a chance for a private talk with his son, Gregers shows deep bitterness toward his father. Accusing Werle of deceit in marrying off Gina to Hialmar, reproaching the lecherous behavior which caused his mother's death, Gregers concludes by blaming his father for ruining old Ekdal's life by framing him for the government swindle. Werle denies this last accusation. He tells his son that he should bury his past grievances and show filial approval for the intended marriage to Mrs. Sorby. It is not fair to his future wife to be a spectacle of scandal, and besides, they are well suited to each other. Gregers laughs scornfully. Never was there any family life in this house, he says, and now for the sake of Mrs. Sorby we are to set up a pretense of harmony, a "tableau of filial affection" to annihilate the last rumors "as to the wrongs the dead mother had to submit to." Pitying the gullibility of "poor Hialmar Ekdal" who does not realize that "what he calls his home is built up on a lie," Gregers says he will leave the house forever "for at last I see my mission in life."

Commentary
Despite the brevity of this act, it lacks the intensity and tension that the introductory scenes build up in the previous plays. Ibsen quickly establishes all the relationships, however, and as he develops the history of his characters he shows which ones are "realistic" (old Werle and Mrs. Sorby, for instance) and which ones are tainted with "idealism" to cover their own weaknesses (Gregers and Hialmar Ekdal).

Mrs. Sorby appears in this act as a woman of the world. Although without status, she is able to treat her influential guests as equals and behaves with frankness (wittily implying that the chamberlains take graft) and compassion (ordering the servant to give "something nice" to old Ekdal to take home).

Hialmar Ekdal exposes his concern for keeping up appearances. At the same time he mourns his father's fallen position in society, he refuses to acknowledge publicly that he is related to the disreputable old man who intrudes on the high class party. Insisting that his wife is "not without education" Hialmar shows his status-seeking aspirations and proves that he has an inflated self-conceit.

The appearance of Lieutenant Ekdal at the party shows the audience his simplicity and lack of self-consciousness. He seems a creature from another world who merely stumbles blindly through those social spheres which include the chamberlains, Mr. Werle, and Mrs. Sorby. According to this scheme, Gregers and Hialmar, who each suspect themselves of being "thirteenth at table," inhabit a peripheral sphere which lies somewhere between the worlds of old Ekdal and old Werle.

ACT II

Summary
The scene takes place in Ekdal's studio. Gina is sewing; her daughter Hedvig peers at a book on the table. They talk desultorily, recounting the costs of food items, the major part of their budget going for butter and beer. Their conversation shows how frugally they live, keeping luxury items for Hialmar's consumption and sacrificing their own cravings for delicacies. Hedvig hopes her father will return soon, for he promised to bring her "something nice" to eat from the dinner party.

When Lieutenant Ekdal returns with a package under his arm and asks no one to disturb him in his room this evening, mother and daughter exchange knowing smiles; they realize the old man intends to spend the evening with his cognac. Hialmar appears and his father emerges to greet him. While the women eagerly help him take his overcoat, they admire how handsome he looks and ask many questions about the party. Hialmar names the guests he consorted with—"Chamberlain Flor and Chamberlain Balle and Chamberlain Kaspersen"—and they are all very impressed. Carried away by his sense of importance, Ekdal represents himself as the most intellectual and vivacious man at the party. He concludes by treating his family to a lecture about the vintages of wine.

Hedvig expectantly eyes her father, but he has not the slightest idea at what she is hinting. Finally she asks him to bring forth the good things he promised. Hialmar confesses that he forgot all about it. "But wait, Hedvig, I do have something for you," he says digging in his pockets while she jumps up and down in happy anticipation. To her disappointment, he brings out the menu, announcing he will read the bill of fare and describe all the rich dishes to her. Seeing how she gulps back her tears, he interrupts his menu reading, angrily complaining about "the absurd things the father of a family is expected to think of" and being treated to "sour faces" when he forgets the smallest trifle.

The wife and daughter dutifully change the subject, but Hialmar still feels like a martyr. To further fill "his cup of bitterness," Ekdal supposes that no one has yet rented their spare room, and he supposes that no new customers have shown up for portrait sittings, and, sighing, concludes he is willing to work "so long as my strength holds out." Hedvig humbly offers him some beer. Waving her away, he says, "I require nothing, nothing." Adding at once "Beer? Was it beer you were talking about?" Hialmar accepts and all four are happy again. Glass in hand, surrounded by his family, Ekdal pronounces his forgiveness. "Our roof may be poor and humble, but it is home," he says. "And with all my heart I say: Here dwells my happiness."

There is a knock on the door, and Gina admits Gregers Werle. During their talk, Hialmar lowers his voice to prevent Hedvig from hearing. The child is in danger of losing her eyesight, he informs Gregers, although only the first symptoms have appeared as yet. The blindness will inexorably develop, for it is a hereditary disease. "Yes," Gina quickly avers, "Ekdal's mother had weak eyes," but Gregers is suspicious.

Gregers turns to greet Lieutenant Ekdal, reminding the old man how he used to be an avid hunter in the days when he worked in the forests. "How can a man like you — such a man for the open air — live in the midst of a stuffy town, boxed within four walls?" asks Gregers. In reply, Ekdal draws young Werle to the door of the garret where skylights admit beams of moonlight to illuminate the darkness of a large room. Proudly the old man shows his guest the barely discernible pigeons, rabbits, especially pointing out their favorite treasure asleep in a basket — a wild duck. Quietly closing the door, old Ekdal tells Gregers that the wild duck was an indirect present from his father, for Werle brought it back wounded from a hunting trip and had asked a servant to get rid of it. After the duck had been shot, Werle's "amazingly clever dog" dived to retrieve it from the depths of the lake:

> They always do that, wild ducks do [continues the old man]. They dive to the bottom as deep as they can get, sir — and bite themselves fast in the tangle and seaweed. And they never come up again.

She thrives wonderfully well in the garret, Hialmar proudly relates. By now the wild duck is so used to it that she has forgotten her natural wild life and "it all depends on that." Nodding, Gregers counsels them to "be sure you never let her get a glimpse of the sky and the sea" for then she will pine for her former freedom.

He surprises them by asking if he may rent their spare room. Hialmar agrees and asks what Gregers plans to do in town:

> I should like best to be an amazingly clever dog [answers young Werle], one that goes to the bottom after wild ducks when they dive and bite themselves fast in tangle and seaweed down among the ooze.

Gregers bids them good-night, proposing to move in the next morning. Old Ekdal has fallen asleep by this time and Gina and Hialmar carry him to bed as the curtain falls.

55

Commentary

In the first act, Ibsen describes the world of Hakon Werle. Not only does the transition to the setting of the second scene provide interesting contrast with the wealthy industrialist's circle, but it implies that Hialmar Ekdal's household is a direct offspring of old Werle's achievements. The Ekdal ménage is possible only because Werle subsidized Ekdal's professional training, provided Hialmar with a wife and child, and even furnished the precious wild duck. This relationship between the two worlds—that of old Werle and that of Hialmar—is significant for it underscores the imitative nature of Hialmar Ekdal's life.

More specifically, the important discovery the audience makes in this act about Hialmar's character is his relationship to Hedvig. Feeling deep love for her father, the child believes he is the great man he pretends to be. However Hialmar is too self-involved to return this love. When he tries to compensate Hedvig's disappointment by presenting her with a bill of fare from the dinner party rather than bringing her a promised tidbit from the table, Hialmar symbolizes his entire way of life. The menu as a substitute for the food, represents how Ekdal substitutes high-sounding phrases for a depth of feeling he cannot achieve.

Having established this point, Ibsen now feels his audience is ready to accept the wild duck, and he introduces the bird as a symbol which gains in complexity as the drama develops. In the first place, the wild duck represents the world of fantasy through which Hialmar and his father compensate for the drabness and mediocrity of their lives. She is the final touch, which, like a work of art that requires at least one realistic detail to make it appear real, brings their hunting ground in the garret to a state of perfection. Gregers, however, has a different interpretation of the wild duck myth. He believes that the bird symbolizes the entire Ekdal family who will drown in the ooze of fantasy and self-delusion. He feels it is his mission to rescue the Ekdals from these dangerous depths, just as his father's dog retrieved the duck from the suffocating seaweed.

ACT III

Summary
It is late the next morning. Gina describes to her husband the havoc Gregers caused in his room. When he tried to put out the fire in the stove, he poured water on it, flooding the whole floor. She leaves him alone to work on retouching photographs. Ekdal's task is constantly interrupted by his father who discusses needed improvements in the garret. Such jobs as moving the watering trough and cutting a path to the duck's basket interest Hialmar, and he is tempted to leave his work. Seeing his divided attention, Hedvig offers to do the retouching for him, even though it might strain her eyes. Hialmar is overcome by the temptation, and he hands her the brush and proofs and joins his father in the attic.

Gregers enters and asks the child many questions. Hedvig informs him that her eyes are now too weak for her to attend school and Hialmar has promised to read with her at home, although he has never had time yet. Gregers also makes Gina uncomfortable by his searching questions. She is forced to admit that she carries on most of the business for her husband; besides having learned to retouch, she also takes the photographs. "You can't expect a man like Ekdal to do nothing but take pictures of Dick, Tom, and Harry," she says. "He's not like one of your common photographers." They hear a shot fired in the garret, and Hialmar emerges, embarrassed when Gregers remarks that "you have become a sportsman, too." Ekdal snappishly replies that he does "a little rabbit shooting now and then, mostly to please father, you understand."

Hialmar asks his wife to prepare lunch. Besides Gregers, he has invited Molvik and Relling, the clergyman and physician who live downstairs, to eat with them. Turning to Gregers, Hialmar now divulges why he leaves the "everyday business details" to Gina: he must "give his mind" to more important things—an invention that will "so exalt" photography that it will become both "an art and a science." It is not for his own sake, he continues, that he pursues this sacred mission. Through his invention he will restore his father's reputation by "restoring the name of Ekdal to honor and dignity." He can give no details about the nature of his invention as yet, but he spends time thinking about it—such work cannot be rushed nor can one be goaded to it, he says. "I almost think you have something of the wild duck in you," Gregers tells him. You have strayed into a "poisonous marsh" and now that "insidious disease has taken hold of you, you have sunk down to die in the dark."

Relling and Molvik arrive just as lunch is ready. The physician remembers Gregers from the Höidal works. "He went around to all the cottars' cabins presenting something he called 'the claim of the ideal,'" Relling tells the company. He wonders whether Gregers has become less idealistic over the years. "Never when I have a true man to deal with," young Werle answers fervently. Changing the subject, Relling cheerfully announces that Molvik was disgustingly drunk the night before. He is demonic, you know, the doctor explains, "and demonic natures are not made to walk straight through the world; they must meander a little now and then."

As they dine, Hialmar makes a maudlin little speech about his devotion to Hedvig and tells Gina she is a "good helpmate on the path of life." Relling turns to Gregers remarking how pleasant to sit at a "well-spread table in a happy family circle." For my part, answers Werle, "I don't thrive in marsh vapors," and Gina is insulted for she gives the house a good airing every day. "No airing you can give will drive out the taint I mean," says Gregers and he leaves the table.

At a sudden knock at the door, old Mr. Werle enters, asking to speak with his son. After everyone discreetly departs, Werle informs Gregers that, with his marriage, his son's share of the property falls to him. Gregers refuses to accept the money; he wants for nothing, he says, and has only his "mission" to fulfill. He wants to cut all ties with his father.

After Werle leaves, Gregers asks Hialmar to join him for a long walk. Dr. Relling bitterly sees them go. "It's a thousand pities the fellow didn't go to hell through one of the Höidal mines," he says aloud. Gina remarks that Werle must be mad; his only disease, says Relling, is an "acute attack of integrity."

58

Commentary

The significant feature of this act is that it establishes the points of opposition between Relling and Gregers. Both men feel responsible for the lives of others, but the physician's "mission" is contrary to that of Gregers. Ibsen shows that the realist is the one who encourages self-deception as a technique of facing life's disappointments (Relling provides Hialmar with an approving audience for Ekdal's empty pronouncements) while the idealist encourages truthfulness as a way to self-fulfillment.

ACT IV

Summary

It is later in the afternoon, and Gina and Hedvig wonder where Hialmar is. Dinner is late, a feature unusual in the Ekdal home. Finally Hialmar arrives, looking tired and worn. They think he is ill because he refuses to eat. He increases their anxiety by announcing that from now on he shall begin to take all the work in his own hands. What about the invention, asks Gina. Hedvig implores, "And think about the wild duck, father, and all the hens and rabbits." He will never set foot in that garret again, Hialmar says; "I should almost like to wring that cursed wild duck's neck!" Hedvig covers her ears. "Oh no, father, you know it's my wild duck," she cries and shakes him. For her sake, Hialmar promises, he shall never harm the bird. After Hedvig goes for her afternoon walk, the husband and wife are able to talk.

Questioning Gina, Hialmar forces her to admit of her previous liaison with old Werle. She was afraid to tell him before their marriage, Gina says, for fear he would change his mind. Now that their home is cozy and happy, more money comes in every day, they can forget about past happenings, she tells him. "This dull callous contentment," rails Hialmar; our home is mired in "the swamp of deceit." While Gina cries, Hialmar morosely observes that his "whole dream has vanished."

Beaming with satisfaction, Gregers confidently enters. Where he expected "the light of transfiguration" to shine from husband and wife, he is surprised to find nothing but "dullness, oppression, and gloom," he says. He cannot understand why Hialmar, with his sensitive perceptiveness, is unable to "feel a new consecration after the great crisis." Relling enters at this point, rudely asking Gregers his purpose in coming here. "To lay the foundations of a true marriage," responds young Werle. The physician reminds them that, although they are free to mess up their lives, they must remember a child is involved. Hedvig is at a critical age, he says, where she has "all sorts of mischief in her head." Hialmar promptly vows he shall protect his child "so long as I am above ground."

At this moment Mrs. Sorby pays them an unexpected visit. About to leave for the Höidal works where she and Werle are to be married, she wishes to say good-bye. Having been a friend of Mrs. Sorby for many years, Dr. Relling announces that he shall mourn his loss during a drinking binge with Molvik this night. Gregers threatens to let his father know of Mrs. Sorby's previous connection with Relling. He knows everything that can be truthfully said about me, answers the housekeeper, nor does he keep any secrets from me. Moreover, she tells Gregers, this marriage is not entirely one-sided; now that your father is going blind he needs someone like me "to stand beside him and care for him." Hialmar is startled. "Going blind?" he says wonderingly. "That's strange. He too going blind." Taking affectionate leave of Gina, Mrs. Sorby exits.

When Hedvig comes in, she shows her father a letter which Mrs. Sorby gave her as a birthday present. Written in Werle's hand, the letter grants a monthly allowance of one hundred crowns to Lieutenant Ekdal, which will, upon the old man's death, continue as a lifelong settlement upon Hedvig. Hialmar draws the shocking conclusion, and sends Hedvig out of the room. He turns to his wife, asking whether or not the child is really his daughter. Gina pleads ignorance and admits she does not know. "Gregers, I have no child!" wails Hialmar, while Hedvig rushes in and embraces her tearful father. He shrinks from her touch. "Keep far away. I cannot bear to see you," he cries. "Oh! Those eyes!" And Hialmar plunges out of the house. Gina tries to comfort her sobbing daughter. Going out to fetch Ekdal, she leaves Gregers and Hedvig alone onstage.

Young Werle suggests that Hedvig sacrifice the wild duck to show her love for her father. This free will offering of "the dearest treasure you have in the world" will provide Hialmar proof of Hedvig's devotion. The child is hopeful and says she will ask her grandfather to shoot the bird for her. Gina comes back, saying that Ekdal had gone out with Relling and Molvik. Gregers wonders that he should go out "this evening, when his mind so sorely needs to wrestle in solitude." The curtain falls as Gina tries to comfort the sobbing Hedvig.

Commentary

In this act, Gregers believes his mission is accomplished. Having disclosed the truth about Hialmar's family, the young Werle looks forward to viewing the process of purification in his friend. The outcome, however, is ironic: in a fit of self-indulgent martyrdom Hialmar rejects his family. Though he has said he will protect his child until he is buried, the father renounces Hedvig as soon as he discovers she is old Werle's daughter. Escaping from the inner conflict this knowledge has aroused, Hialmar goes off on a drinking binge with Relling and Volvik.

Gregers, however, still believes that his friend is capable of laying the foundations of a new life. He now carries his "claim of the ideal" to Hedvig. Gregers believes that if she would show her love by sacrificing the wild duck, Ekdal will recognize the value of his family ties. He furthermore thinks that once the wild duck is destroyed, the Ekdal household will be freed from the curse of delusion and fantasy. By this train of thought Gregers unwittingly commits the same logical error he tries to make Hialmar avoid: he acts on the belief that if the symbol of fantasy is effaced, then the Ekdals' lives will be devoted to a truthful acceptance of their lot.

ACT V

Summary
Cold, gray morning light illuminates the stage, and Hialmar has not returned. Dr. Relling informs them he is asleep on the sofa in his apartment. "How can he sleep?" asks the despairing Hedvig, and Gregers answers that the man needs rest after "the spiritual conflict which has rent him." Relling differs, observing that he noticed no such tumult in Hialmar. When Gina and Hedvig are out of the

room, Gregers says he is amazed that Relling cannot see the great-
ness of Hialmar Ekdal's character. Raised by hysterical maiden
aunts, replies the physician, Hialmar only passed as a great man. His
father "who has been an ass all his days" approved of everything
the young man did. The doctor continues:

> But then when our dear sweet Hialmar went to college he at
> once passed for the great light of the future amongst his com-
> rades too! He was handsome, the rascal—red and white—a
> shopgirl's dream of manly beauty; and with his superficially
> emotional temperament and his sympathetic voice for declaim-
> ing other people's verses and other people's thoughts—[Here
> Gregers interrupts angrily.]

The physician begins to diagnose young Werle. "You, who are always in a delirium of hero worship," are sick. You must always
have something outside yourself to adore, and Gregers admits the
truth of Relling's observations. Relling tells young Werle that in
Hialmar's case of sickness he applies the "usual remedy": "I am
cultivating the life illusion in him," says the physician. As
for Molvik, "since the harmless creature would have succumbed
to self-contempt and despair" long ago, Relling, by way of cure,
invented his being "demonic." Old Ekdal has found his own remedy,
for "there is not a happier sportsman in the world than that old man
pottering about" in the garret. Gregers agrees that the unfortunate
old man has "indeed had to narrow the ideals of his youth." Don't
use that foreign word "ideals," Relling retorts. "We have the excellent native word: lies." Gregers vows to rest only after he has freed
Hialmar from the doctor's clutches. "Rob the average man of his life
illusion and you rob him of his happiness at the same stroke," warns
Relling before he goes. With a final word to Hedvig to remind her
that the "fearless spirit of sacrifice" would recall her father, Gregers
also exits.

"How would you go about shooting a duck, grandfather?" the
child asks as Lieutenant Ekdal emerges from the garret. In the
breast, against the feathers, he answers, and retires into his room.
Hedvig gingerly takes the double-barrelled pistol from the shelf,
hastily replacing it when Gina enters. Her mother bids her prepare a

breakfast tray for father; suddenly Hialmar appears, bleary-eyed and dishevelled. The child cries out for joy, but he turns away, telling Gina, "Keep her away from me, I say." Hedvig disappears without a word.

Hialmar asks his wife to pack his clothes for he intends to leave and "my helpless father will come with me." Searching for his papers in Hedvig's room, he cruelly orders her out. In my last moments in this my former home, Ekdal tells Gina, "I wish to be spared from interlopers." Hedvig stands alone onstage, fighting back her tears. Thinking of the wild duck, she takes the pistol and softly steals into the garret.

Meanwhile Hialmar, complaining about "the exhausting preparations" for leaving, sits down to his coffee, munching on heavily buttered bread. As Gina points out how difficult it will be to find accommodations for the birds and pigeons which his father needs, Hialmar decides to stay at home for a day or so until an available apartment turns up. He also decides to save the letter from Werle; he says it really belongs to father and he had no right to tear it up. Gregers enters at this point to find Hialmar gluing the torn pieces of paper together. He is disappointed to find Ekdal ready to leave the house and reminds him of the invention he must finish. There is no invention, answers Hialmar bitterly; it was all Relling's idea, and he continued to think of it because it made Hedvig so happy. "How unutterably I loved the child," moans the father, and now I begin to doubt that perhaps she has never honestly loved me. Hearing the duck quacking in the garret, Hialmar believes his father is hunting in there, but Gregar's face shows joy as he says that Hialmar may yet have proof of Hedvig's love. Continuing his dark thoughts, Ekdal asserts that, since she faces a rich future, the wealth will turn her head and Hedvig will surely leave him:

> If I then asked her [he goes on], 'Hedvig, are you willing to renounce that life for me?' ...you would soon hear what answer I should get.

A pistol shot rings out from the garret. Gina rushes in, worried that the old man is shooting by himself. Excitedly Gregers explains that Hedvig had her grandfather shoot the bird for if she sacrificed her most cherished possession "then you would surely come to love her again." When old Ekdal looks out from his room, they have a sudden foreboding, and rush into the garret. Hialmar and Gregers carry Hedvig to the sofa, and Relling, having come when called, pronounces her dead. Gina sobs and reaches for her husband. "We must help each other to bear it, for now she belongs to us both," she says.

Relling gazes searchingly at Gregers; the death was no accident, he declares accusingly. "Hedvig has not died in vain," young Werle asserts. "Did you not see how sorrow set free what was noble in Hialmar?" That is only temporary, answers the doctor. Within a year, Hedvig "will be nothing to him but a pretty theme for declamation." Hialmar shall soon steep himself in a "syrup of sentiment and self-admiration and self-pity," Relling tells the shocked Gregers. If you are right, then life is not worth living, the young man tells him:

Life would be quite tolerable after all [says the physician] if only we could get rid of the confounded duns that keep pestering us in our poverty with the claims of the ideal.

In that case, says Gregers as he prepares to go, I am glad for my destiny — "to be thirteenth at table." "The devil it is," mutters Relling as the curtain rings down.

Commentary
Life would be quite tolerable, Relling says as he expresses the keynote of the play, if imperfect souls do not destroy themselves by trying to meet the claims of the ideal. Unable to accept this doctrine as an acceptable standard of life, Gregers chooses to be "thirteenth at table" — to remain outside the circle of the normal human condition. Hialmar, on the other hand, lacking personal integrity, will survive because he can easily build up a new series of self-deceptions to overcome temporary disillusion. He and Gina will continue their life together, sustaining their sense of personal worth with fresh fantasies.

GENERAL ANALYSIS

The Wild Duck represents an investigation of a problem that Ibsen wrestled with throughout his life. Always concerned with "the claim of the ideal" and proselytizing this claim to others, Ibsen, on the other hand, found in himself qualities of material indulgence and a weakness for worldly recognition. He suspected that he himself, like Gregers, substituted a missionary zeal to reform others for a failure to actively fight for the reforms he desired.

Thus *The Wild Duck* represents a personal compromise for Ibsen. From the problems of self-fulfillment he considered in *A Doll's House* and *Ghosts,* to the cult of the lone strong-willed individual in *Enemy of the People* (produced two years before *The Wild Duck*), Ibsen confronted the logical outcome of a situation where an idealist carries his message as an intrusion on the normal world of mediocrity and hollowness of soul. *The Wild Duck,* in a sense, solved Ibsen's own moral dilemma as he struggled between a militant idealism (as in *Brand* and *Enemy of the People*) and his own worldly temperament. With a pragmatic, anti-romantic viewpoint, this drama presents a continuum between the opposing values of the Ideal and the Real.

By including many symbols in the play that refer to his personal memories, Ibsen provides further evidence that proves *The Wild Duck* is an outcome of his personal struggles. Hedvig, who stands between Gregers' idealism and Hialmar's romantic self-deceptions, is the name of Ibsen's favorite sister. Providing Ibsen with his only family contact, she was deeply religious and tried to imbue her brother with her mystic beliefs. Hedvig, who tells Gregers she reads from an old picture book called *The History of London,* represents Ibsen's mysticism. As a small child he too was fascinated by this same book mentioned in the play, whose illustrations of castles and churches and sailboats bore his thoughts to romantic far off places. Hedvig says the book was left by an old sea captain whom they call "the Flying Dutchman," and this too is true of the book Ibsen had as a child. The "captain," a native of the town of Risör, had been first enslaved in the Barbary states and then imprisoned in England. He died the year Ibsen was born, and the author invested all his romantic dreams in this unknown tragic figure.

STRUCTURE, TECHNIQUE, AND THEME

The Wild Duck's thematic duality—reality versus idealism—becomes a structural feature of the play. Each scene illustrates this dualism. First Gregers confronts his father, a realist, and accuses him of a life built on lies and deception. In the following scene, Gregers confronts Hialmar and begins to rescue his friend from a life of self-delusion. Act III represents the antagonism between the realist Relling and young Werle, while Act IV exposes the paradox between Gregers' principles and the impossibility of realizing them. In the final scene, the duality becomes rationalized with Hedvig's suicide indicating the failure of applying pure principles to inappropriate situations. In effect, Ibsen concludes that life is a dynamic process whose only truth is based on any system which supports an individual's will to survive; life cannot exist according to principle but according to a compromise between emotional needs and the environment.

The central symbol of the play—an image borrowed from romanticism—further illustrates this duality. Ironically Ibsen uses it to destroy the very romanticism he describes in his characters. In a little poem called "The Sea Bird," written by Welhaven, one of Norway's most famous romantic poets, a wild duck dies from the shot of a careless hunter and dives silently to the bottom of the sea. Halvdan Koht, an Ibsen biographer, expresses one aspect of the double-viewed meaning of the symbol:

The broken-winged duck [he writes] which gathered around it the dreams in the Ekdal home sent a strange tremulous flute note into the harsh, cold realism which otherwise gave such a sinister air to the play.

The "sinister air" Koht refers to is the resolution between the shabby, unromantic atmosphere of Ekdal's household and Hialmar's fantasy life expressed by the wilderness hunting ground in the garret, the hopes of Hedvig and their realization, and Ekdal's imitative life-values with his imaginary invention.

Ibsen furthermore expresses the paradoxical nature of life with his use of humor. Although the Ekdal household is a tragic one, eventually sacrificing Hedvig to Hialmar's personal emptiness, the comedy of the situation is unmistakable and serves to heighten the seriousness of Ibsen's theme. Hialmar's affections, his poses, his ridiculous interest in richly buttered bread and cold beer are not in themselves funny; these qualities underscore the pathetic mediocrity of his character. Gregers Werle, as well, ascetic and grimly serious about his "life's mission," is ridiculous when he proves his worldly ineptness by smoking up his room from a badly-fired stove, then flooding the floor to douse the fire. Molvik, the romantic clergyman who saves face by considering himself "demonic" is a funny character. Again this humorous quality serves a serious purpose. With Molvik, Ibsen ironically subverts the efficacy of Relling's romantic remedies of the "life-lies": at the side of Hedvig's corpse, Molvik's inappropriate declamation, "the child is not dead but sleepeth," underscores the pathetic futility of trying to avoid, by various methods, the tragic consequences of human frailty.

Using humor as a technique to indicate the tragic paradox between living according to principles of reality or ideality, and using dialogue and situations to underline the duality, Ibsen's *The Wild Duck* shows that life-truths are dynamic processes which sustain individuals according to their human weaknesses. According to this system, "life-lies" are life-truths, an idealistic point of view leads to self-deception, and "truth" is whatever belief an individual requires to sustain life.

CHARACTERS AND SYMBOLS

As in all of Ibsen's plays, the characters in *The Wild Duck* reflect each other and by mutual comparison amplify the dramatic theme and hasten events to their conclusion. In this play, however, the characters are not only related among themselves; they each bear relation to the integral symbolism of the play, especially the image of the wild duck. Only old Werle and Mrs. Sorby are excepted. Facing realities in their past and present, these pragmatic individuals successfully begin to build a life based on mutual trust and truthfulness. Werle, in fact, desired that his servant get rid of the wounded bird: he has no need of a wild duck.

Hedvig, the innocent victim of the tension between the two men who stand for the "lie" and the "truth" has much in common with the wild duck. Too inexperienced to recognize the shallow affection Hialmar accords her, she is happy at home, for, like the wild duck who has forgotten the freedom of sky, sea, and woods in captivity, she has had no contrasting experience in life to provide her with perspective on those she lives with. Moreover, since she is Gina's natural daughter, she, like the wounded bird, is an indirect present from old Werle to the Ekdals. When Hedvig realizes that her father rejects her, she plans to sacrifice the wild duck to show her love and recall his. This is her attempt to adjust to the new truth Gregers has revealed. Finding her free will offering insufficient, however, Hedvig goes one step further and kills herself. With this suicide, the wild duck and Hedvig become joined: she dies in lieu of the bird as if to prove Gregers' warning that the wild duck, after once glimpsing the blue sky, will pine for her former freedom. Hedvig, with a glimpse of the truth of her father's feelings for her, dies because she cannot bear to live with the knowledge of her origins.

Gregers Werle, appearing as a bird of ill omen, tries to rescue the Ekdals from the swamp of their self-deception. He thinks Hialmar a wounded bird who will drown in the depths of the sea unless Gregers, like his father's "amazingly clever dog," will dive to retrieve him. However, he soon discovers his own self-deception. Encountering failure at proclaiming the truth, discovering his admired friend Hialmar to be a hollow-souled egotist, Gregers recognizes that lies are necessary to existence. Unwilling, however, to accept this pragmatic solution to life, Gregers himself becomes like the wild duck, who, when wounded, bites fast to the underwater seaweed and drowns: despite the ruined dreams, he still clings to the illusory "claim of the ideal." Despairing to find a worthwhile way of life, he dooms himself to be "thirteenth at table"—an uncompromising tenacity to principle which can only end in suicide.

Where Gregers proves to be an unsuccessful retriever, Dr. Relling is successful. Like Werle's "amazingly clever dog" the physician rescues individuals from the "marsh poisons" of their unfulfilled desires. By providing these wounded "wild ducks" with a new environment in their imaginations, he encourages his friends to adjust to the unsatisfactory circumstances of life. His romanticism thus generates the very force for men of weak character to maintain their hold on reality.

Another significant symbolic idea in *The Wild Duck* is that of photography. That Hialmar Ekdal is a photographer underscores the imitative nature of his way of life. Taking ideas and ideals from other sources, Hialmar presents an image of nobility and an appearance of character depth he does not really possess. In the course of the play, Hialmar is busy at retouching — we never see him take any pictures. By the same token, Ekdal retouches his own self-image, minimizing his character blemishes until his whole life is a distortion of the truth.

CHARACTER ANALYSIS

Gregers Werle

Gregers Werle is the son of a man he detests and he has avoided his father by spending the past fifteen years in the family mining concern, the Höidal works, in the northern forests of Norway. In the course of the play Ibsen establishes that, because he is so unattractive in appearance, Gregers has abandoned the hope of settling down with his own family; his long brooding solitude has prevented him, furthermore, from understanding his father. Young Werle, an idealist, feels that his mission is to Advocate & Preach Truth and Purity of Soul whenever he can. In the events of *The Wild Duck,* Gregers plays a major role of proving to others the virtues of the "claim of the ideal."

Hakon Werle

The old man himself, Hakon Werle, has allegedly driven his sick wife to her death by carrying on love affairs in his own home. First he caused his young serving girl, Gina, to become pregnant. Arranging her marriage with Hialmar Ekdal, the son of his former partner, Werle also provided money for the young man to take up the profession of photography. Hialmar is pleased with his marriage and believes that Gina's child is his own daughter, now fourteen years old. At present, Werle lives with his housekeeper, Mrs. Sorby, and intends to marry her. Both have no secrets about their past life and have exposed to each other all their previous connections.

Lieutenant Ekdal

Werle's former partner is now a broken old man. He does odd jobs of copy work for Werle's bookkeeper which provides him with enough means to buy an occasional bottle of cognac. Fourteen years ago, when old Ekdal was active at the Höidal works, the company appropriated a large quantity of lumber from government-owned land. Ekdal paid for this crime by serving a jail sentence and losing his reputation. He now lives with Hialmar and Gina.

The other characters bear brief mention. *Dr. Relling*, the realist of the play, lives in a downstairs apartment from the Ekdals. His roommate is *Molvik*, a weak-charactered clergyman. *Hedvig*, Ekdal's adolescent daughter, is the sensitive innocent who suffers the most in this drama of misapplied idealism.

DRAMA OF IBSEN

Although the plays are interesting for their social message, Ibsenite drama would not survive today were it not for his consummate skill as a technician. Each drama is carefully wrought into a tight logical construction where characters are clearly delineated and interrelated, and where events have a symbolic as well as actual significance. The symbolism in Ibsen's plays is rarely overworked. Carefully integrated to unify the setting, events, and character portrayals, the symbols are incidental and subordinate to the truth and consistency of his picture of life.

Having been interested in studying painting as a youth, Ibsen was always conscious of making accurate observations. As a dramatist, he considered himself a photographer as well, using his powers of observation as a lens, while his finished plays represented the proofs of a skilled darkroom technician. The realism of his plays, the credibility of his characters, the immediacy of his themes attest to these photographic skills at which Ibsen so consciously worked. Among his countless revisions for each drama, he paid special heed to the accuracy of his dialogue. Through constant rewriting, he brought out the maximum meaning in the fewest words, attempting to fit each speech into the character of the speaker. In addition, Ibsen's ability as a poet contributed a special beauty to his terse prose.

The problems of Ibsen's social dramas are consistent throughout all his works. George Brandes, a contemporary critic, said of Ibsen, as early as the 1860s, that "his progress from one work to the other is not due to a rich variety of themes and ideas, but on the contrary to a perpetual scrutiny of the same general questions, regarded from different points of view." In *A Doll's House,* he especially probed the problems of the social passivity assigned to women in a male-oriented society. After considering the plight of Nora Helmer, he then investigated what would happen had she remained at home. The consequence of his thoughts appears as *Ghosts.* Going one step further, Ibsen investigated the fallacies inherent in his own idealism. Much as Pastor Manders applies empty principles to actual situations Gregers Werle is shown trying to impose an idealistic viewpoint when circumstances demand that individuals can only accept their lives by clinging to "life-lies." Although *The Wild Duck* differs in treatment from *Hedda Gabler,* the plays both have protagonists who find in their imaginations an outlet for their frustrations. *Hedda Gabler,* however, with its emphasis on individual psychology, is a close scrutiny of a woman like Nora Helmer or Mrs. Alving who searches for personal meaning in a society which denies freedom of expression.

Professor Koht, a renown scholar, sums up the dramatist's investigations:

> The thing which filled [Ibsen's] mind was the individual man, and he measured the worth of a community according as it helped or hindered a man in being himself. He had an ideal standard which he placed upon the community and it was from this measuring that his social criticism proceeded.

Secondary to, and in connection with, his idea that the individual is of supreme importance, Ibsen believed that the final personal tragedy comes from a denial of love. From this viewpoint we see that Torvald is an incomplete individual because he attaches more importance to a crime against society than a sin against love. The same is true for Pastor Manders. Hedda Gabler is doomed to a dissatisfied life because she too is unable to love, and Hedvig's tragic suicide is the result of her pathetic attempt to recall her father's affections. In Ibsen's other plays, particularly *Brand,* this theme is of primary importance.

In an age when nations were striving for independence, Ibsen's sense of democracy was politically prophetic. He believed, not that "right" was the preogative of the mass majority, but that it resided among the educated minority. In the development and enrichment of the individual, he saw the only hope of a really cultured and enlightened society.

IBSEN'S CONTRIBUTIONS TO THE THEATER

Until the latter part of the nineteenth century, theater remained a vehicle of entertainment. Insights into the human condition were merely incidental factors in the dramatist's art. Ibsen, however, contributed a new significance to drama which changed the development of modern theater. Discovering dramatic material in everyday situations was the beginning of a realism that novelists as different as Zola and Flaubert were already exploiting. When Nora quietly confronts her husband with "Sit down, Torvald, you and I have much to say to each other," drama became no longer a mere diversion, but an experience closely impinging on the lives of the playgoers themselves. With Ibsen, the stage became a pulpit, while the dramatist exhorting his audience to reassess the values of society, became the minister of a new social responsibility.

COMPLETE LIST OF IBSEN'S DRAMAS

VERSE 1850 Catiline
1850 The Warrior's Barrow
1853 St. John's Night
1855 Lady Inger of Ostratt
1856 The Feast of Solhaug
1857 Olaf Liljekrans
1858 The Vikings of Helgeland

1862 Love's Comedy
1864 The Pretenders
1866 Brand
1867 Peer Gynt
1873 Emperor and Galilean (blank verse)

PROSE 1869 The League of Youth
1877 The Pillars of Society
1879 A Doll's House
1881 Ghosts
1882 An Enemy of the People
1884 The Wild Duck
1886 Rosmersholm
1888 The Lady from the Sea
1890 Hedda Gabler
1892 The Master Builder
1894 Little Eyolf
1896 John Gabriel Borkman
1900 When We Dead Awaken

SELECTED BIBLIOGRAPHY

Brian W. Downs, *A Study of Six Plays by Ibsen;* Cambridge, England: 1950.

Edmund Gosse, *Henrik Ibsen;* London: 1907.

Halvdan Koht, *The Life of Ibsen,* translated by R. L. McMahon and H. A. Larsen; 2 vols.; New York: 1931.

Janko Lavrin, *Ibsen, An Approach;* London: 1950.

M. S. Moses, *Henrik Ibsen, the Man and His Plays;* Boston: 1920.

George Bernard Shaw, *The Quintessence of Ibsenism;* Ayot St. Lawrence edition, vol. 19; London: 1921.

Hermann J. Wiegand, *The Modern Ibsen;* New York: 1925.

Adolph Edouard Zucker, *Ibsen, the Master Builder;* New York: 1929.

QUESTIONS FOR DISCUSSION

1. Using specific examples, discuss how Ibsen's "progress from one work to the other" is due to "a perpetual scrutiny of the same general questions regarded from different points of view."

2. Do you feel that Ibsen's drama is "dated"? To defend your view, cite dramatic themes in these plays which you consider to be universal, or limited in scope.

3. Often considered grim and oppressive, Ibsen's social dramas always contain considerable humor. From your own reading of these three plays, discuss the scenes which a comedy-conscious stage manager would be most likely to exploit for humor.

4. At least one character in each of these plays prefers his imaginary view of life to a realistic viewpoint. With this in mind, discuss the life-views of Pastor Manders, Hialmar Ekdal, and Dr. Stockmann.

5. What additional insight into the following characters does their choice of vocation provide: Hialmar Ekdal—photographer; Oswald Alving—painter; Dr. Stockmann—medical doctor?

6. For each of the three plays, show how the first act forewarns the audience of almost all the forthcoming events in the rest of the drama.

7. Point out some instances where Ibsen is able to "externalize" inner problems by using effective symbols. (Example: Oswald's physical disease which stands for a morally diseased society.)

8. What are the "ghosts" in *Ghosts?* Discuss some "ghosts" of contemporary society to which we, as individuals or as a nation, still succumb.

9. In your own words, explain why Dr. Relling prefers "the excellent native word—lies" to the word "ideals."

10. Discuss the relationship *The Wild Duck* bears to Ibsen's dramatic development.

11. Explain the symbolic significance of hereditary disease in *Ghosts*.

NOTES

NOTES

NOTES

NOTES

NOTES

NOTES